Pharaohs in Skirts. Egyptian Mythology for Teens

The Formidable Females Behind the Legends of Ancient Egypt's Goddesses, Queens, and Leaders

Terri Gallagher

© **Copyright 2024 - All rights reserved.**

The content contained within this book may not be reproduced, duplicated or transmitted without direct written permission from the author or the publisher.

Under no circumstances will any blame or legal responsibility be held against the publisher, or author, for any damages, reparation, or monetary loss due to the information contained within this book, either directly or indirectly.

Legal Notice:

This book is copyright protected. It is only for personal use. You cannot amend, distribute, sell, use, quote or paraphrase any part, or the content within this book, without the consent of the author or publisher.

Disclaimer Notice:

Please note the information contained within this document is for educational and entertainment purposes only. All effort has been executed to present accurate, up to date, reliable, complete information. No warranties of any kind are declared or implied. Readers acknowledge that the author is not engaged in the rendering of legal, financial, medical or professional advice. The content within this book has been derived from various sources. Please consult a licensed professional before attempting any techniques outlined in this book.

By reading this document, the reader agrees that under no circumstances is the author responsible for any losses, direct or indirect, that are incurred as a result of the use of the information contained within this document, including, but not limited to, errors, omissions, or inaccuracies.

Table of Contents

INTRODUCTION 1

CHAPTER 1: THE WORLD OF WOMEN IN ANCIENT EGYPT 5

    FREEDOM AND FINANCES 6
        Making That Paper 7
        Helping Build the Economy 7
        Barriers Abroad 7
        Patriarchy for Who? 8
    HOUSE AND HOME 9
        Social Standing 9
        Teaching the Children 10
        Mediating Marriages 10
        Helping Each Other Out 10
    WOMEN IN EVERY ROLE 11
        Scribes 11
        Doctors and Healers 12
        Artisans 12
        Positions of Power 13
        Brewers and Launderers 13
    A DAY IN THE LIFE 14
        The Local Baker 14
        The Priestess 14
        The Businesswoman 15
    BE INSPIRED 15
    CONCLUSION 16

CHAPTER 2: DIVINE INFLUENCERS—GODDESSES OF ANCIENT EGYPT 19

    ISIS: PROTECTOR AND LEADER 20
        Lessons We Can Learn From Isis 20
        Modern Influence 22
    BASTET: THE GUARDIAN 23
        The Divine Cat 24
        The Feasts of Bubastis 24
        Modern Influence 24
    SEKHMET: THE GODDESS OF WAR 26
        The Healer 26
        Collective Manifestation 26

- *The Lioness* 27
- LESSER-KNOWN GODDESSES 27
  - *Hathor* 27
  - *Ma'at* 28
  - *Neith* 28
  - *Rituals Performed to Honor These Goddesses* 29
- CONCLUSION 29

CHAPTER 3: RULING BEYOND GENDER—THE FEMALE PHARAOHS............ 31

- SOBEKNEFERU 32
  - *Redefining Power* 32
  - *The Innovative Architect* 33
  - *Sobekneferu's Legacy* 33
- HATSHEPSUT 34
  - *Making a Statement* 35
  - *The Savvy Economist* 36
  - *The Power of Perception* 36
  - *What We Can Learn* 36
- NEFERTITI 37
  - *A New Type of Queen* 38
  - *A New God* 38
  - *A New Kind of Power* 39
- CLEOPATRA VII 39
  - *A Woman of the People* 40
  - *A Powerful Alliance* 40
  - *Misrepresented and Misunderstood* 41
  - *Cleopatra's Legacy* 41
- CONCLUSION 42

CHAPTER 4: QUEENS AT THE HELM—POWER BEYOND THE THRONE 43

- QUEEN TIYE 44
  - *The Diplomat* 44
  - *A Strategic Alliance* 45
  - *Tiye's Legacy* 45
- QUEEN NEFERTARI 46
  - *Nefertari's Temple* 46
  - *Mistress of Upper and Lower Egypt* 47
  - *Women Shaping History* 47
  - *Nefertari's Legacy* 48
- ANKHESENAMUN 49
  - *The Backstory* 49
  - *Check Mate* 50
  - *Ankhesenamun's Legacy* 50
- CONCLUSION 51

CHAPTER 5: WARRIORS AND LEADERS—LEADING WITH COURAGE 53

Ahhotep I 54
- Leading From the Front 54
- A Lesson in Resilience 55
- Ahhotep I's Legacy 55

Neithhotep 56
- Underappreciated by History 57
- Neithhotep's Legacy 57

Nitocris 58
- Separating Fact From Fiction 59
- Nitocris's Legacy 60

Conclusion 61

CHAPTER 6: UNRAVELING SCIENTIFIC MYSTERIES 63

How DNA Studies Help Us Understand Royal Lineages 64
- The Ties That Bind 64
- The Missing Link 65

How Mummy Research Has Affected Knowledge of Women's Health 67
- A Glimpse Into the Unknown 68
- Ancient Nutrition 68
- Embalming Practices 69

How Science Challenges Previous Narratives 70
- Redefining Gender Roles 70
- Using Multiple Approaches 71
- Influence on Modern Perceptions 71

Conclusion 72

CHAPTER 7: SPIRITUAL LIVES—WOMEN IN RELIGION AND BELIEF 75

Priestesses: The Temple Activities 76
- Conduits for the Gods 77
- The Chosen Ones 77
- An Exclusive Club 78

The Influence of Female Oracles 79
- Guidance From the Gods 79
- A Cut Above the Rest 80

The Isis Cult 80
- Isis Goes Viral 81

Conclusion 82

CHAPTER 8: LOVE, PASSION, AND POWER DYNAMICS 83

Cultural Beliefs About Love Stories and Romance 84
- The Tale of Two Brothers 85
- Love Brings Balance 85

 Symbols of Love *86*
POETRY *88*
MARRIAGE RITES AND SOCIAL EXPECTATIONS FOR WOMEN *89*
 The Big Day *90*
 The Dutiful Wife *90*
 Untying the Knot *90*
LGBTQ+ RELATIONSHIPS *91*
 Sexuality Was Fluid *93*
 Different Standards Based on Status *93*
 Humanizing the Gods *93*
CONCLUSION *94*

CHAPTER 9: STORIES AND SYMBOLS—WOMEN IN ART AND LITERATURE 97

FEMALE ARTISTS AND THEIR IMPACT *99*
 Merit Ptah: A Pioneer of Female Artistry *99*
 A Legacy of Defiance *100*
THE EVOLVING PORTRAYAL OF WOMEN IN ARTWORKS *101*
SYMBOLISM IN ART *102*
 The Papyrus and the Lotus *103*
 Deciphering Symbols Focused on Women's Roles *104*
 Influence on Modern Art *106*
FAMOUS FEMALE POETS AND THEIR LEGACY *107*
 Giving Women a Voice *107*
 Common Themes *107*
 Influence of Female Poets *108*
CONCLUSION *109*

CHAPTER 10: STANDARDS OF BEAUTY AND FASHION 111

CULTURAL IMPLICATIONS OF MAKEUP *112*
 Kohl *113*
 Perfumed Oils *113*
 Colored Cosmetics *113*
 A Shared Language *114*
HAIRSTYLING AND USE OF WIGS *115*
 Wigs *115*
 Spiritual Significance *115*
CLOTHING STYLES *116*
 Fashionable Fabrics *117*
 Designs *117*
 Wearing a Masterpiece *117*
SYMBOLIC MESSAGES THROUGH FASHION *118*
 Jewelry and Social Class *118*
 Jewelry and Spirituality *119*
 That's So Last Season *119*

> *Artisans Through the Ages* *119*
> *Cultural Exchange* *120*
>
> CONCLUSION 121

CONCLUSION 123

GLOSSARY 125

AUTHOR BIO 133

REFERENCES 135

> IMAGE REFERENCES 143

Introduction

Once upon a time, in the land of pyramids and pharaohs, where the scorching sun kissed the Nile and camels weren't just part of the exotic scenery but a mode of transport, lived women who were nothing short of incredible. You might already know Cleopatra's name, but history is brimming with so many more powerful female figures whose stories have barely ever been told. Now, you must be wondering—weren't ancient societies deeply patriarchal? Weren't women confined to spinning yarn and managing household chores? Spoiler alert: Ancient Egypt was way ahead of its time when it came to gender dynamics.

Ancient Egyptians lived in an age where women could own land, take their neighbors to court, or even start a business. Yes, you read that right! Plus, they could rock the crown just as fiercely as any male ruler. Whether it was weaving elaborate linens or navigating complex treaties, these women wielded influence in ways we're still trying to figure out.

If you've been scrolling through your Instagram feed and pondering which filter best matches your #empowerment post, then join me in taking a step back and diving into an era and a region where queens ruled hearts and minds just as fiercely as they did kingdoms. Enter Hatshepsut, a woman who asked, "Why should boys have all the fun of being Pharaoh?" and donned the ceremonial beard, not because she had a flair for facial hair fashion but to solidify her claim to power. She didn't just break the glass ceiling; she shattered stone columns while she was at it.

You're probably dealing with situations today where you feel like your strengths are being overlooked. Maybe it's a teacher who doesn't see your potential or societal norms that are holding you back. Think of Hatshepsut standing tall against the tide of tradition, claiming her place, standing on business, and slaying with style. Channeling that kind of

1

courage might just help you navigate your own challenges with newfound resolve.

And then there's Sobekneferu, whose name itself means beauty. When she ascended the throne, she didn't shy away from asserting her capabilities. Her bold determination to be defined by her deeds rather than her gender resonates with the same energy you might find in modern boardrooms or activist circles where women are fighting for equality today. Her example reminds us that leadership transcends gender roles, a lesson as crucial now as it was thousands of years ago.

Let's not forget the everyday heroines, too, like the merchants selling their wares in bustling markets, their voices commanding respect. Think of the vibrant scenes of open-air trade where women weaved through stalls, buying, selling, and making decisions that affected entire communities. In their actions, power wasn't just a dream but a daily reality. Doesn't this make you reflect on how you're paving your own path, one decision at a time?

Picture yourself living in this ancient land, with the vivid scenes of Egyptian life unfolding around you: festivals with dancers swirling in colorful robes, music creating rhythms that pulse through crowds. Even amid such vibrancy, there were struggles—political intrigue, family feuds—but through it all, women maintained their enigmatic poise, teaching lessons in resilience and adaptability that we're still learning from today.

So, what does all this mean for you, the reader? As you'll soon see, this journey is not just about flipping through pages discussing ancient murals and hieroglyphic tales. It's about finding pieces of yourself within each chapter, drawing parallels between the triumphs and trials of these women and your own life. It's about discovering how their stories can inspire yours.

In our quest for empowerment, we often look for role models who mirror our ideals and aspirations. Here lies a treasure trove of extraordinary figures reflecting diversity in leadership, wisdom in decision-making, and balance in personal and professional realms. As you walk through the hallways of the past, filled with echoes of laughter and whispers of secret histories, consider this: The queens and commoners of ancient Egypt did so much more than just survive—they laid the foundational stones for your generation.

From learning to lead like Nefertiti to embracing intellect like Hypatia, your adventure through these chapters will help kindle the fire of determination in your spirit. History isn't just a series of events long past; it's alive, dynamic, and pulsating with relevance. Through the exploration you're about to embark on, you will discover new dimensions of leadership, enhance your self-worth, and find the courage to overcome your personal struggles.

Buckle up for an odyssey across sand-swept landscapes. Peppered with wit and wisdom, every story unfolds another layer of strength, sass, and significance. Welcome to a world where ancient meets modern, where legends live on not just in scripts but in the spirit of young women like you, ready to conquer worlds—one laugh, one hope, and one dream at a time.

Chapter 1:

The World of Women in Ancient Egypt

Understanding the world of women in ancient Egypt is rather like unwrapping a gift with many layers. On the surface, you might see only the golden glow of pyramids and the intrigue of mummies, but tucked away is the fascinating and vivid life of women who knew how to rule their roost while occasionally giving Cleopatra a run for her money. These dynamos weren't just busy baking bread by the Nile or picking out hieroglyphs to adorn the walls of their mudbrick homes. They were way more than the characters lurking in the background of history.

Women's contributions far exceeded shopping for dinner ingredients in bustling marketplaces. Their presence was as noticeable as a sphinx on a grocery run, as they wielded the kind of economic power that would have raised eyebrows in other ancient societies. They managed financial affairs, owned businesses, and probably kept track of which nobles owed them a couple of goats from last year's harvest.

So, why does this chapter matter to us today? Well, it's like flipping through an Instagram feed of ancient Egypt and finding a hashtag that says #girlswithgoals. We're about to shine a light on the rights and freedoms of ancient Egyptian women, covering everything from the legal contracts they managed to the pottery workshops where they contributed more than just the tea for breaks.

You'll also discover the strategic powers that women displayed within their family dynamics, ensuring that the lineage stayed as strong as the stones of the pyramids. Plus, they also occupied diverse professional roles: These formidable females were scribes, doctors, artisans, and more. Each page is filled with tales of independence, influence, and perhaps a little bit of magic. So, gear up to go back in time and meet women who paved their paths long before modern GPS was there to show them the way. Let's explore how they wrote the book on empowerment, one papyrus at a time.

Freedom and Finances

Unlike many societies where women's roles were often confined to the household, Egyptian women wielded significant economic freedom.

Their ability to own, inherit, and manage property set them apart and provided a framework for financial independence—a foundation not commonly afforded to women elsewhere at the time.

Making That Paper

Picture a busy marketplace where women with sharp gazes survey the goods. In this vibrant atmosphere, they were not passive observers. Instead, they actively participated in business transactions and were dynamic players in trade and commerce. This involvement was a way for them to carve out personal wealth and social standing, as the legal system of ancient Egypt recognized women's capability to enter into contracts and manage their affairs without needing a man to hold their hand. Their independence on this front was, according to scholars, a right firmly embedded in daily life (McGee & Moore, 2014).

Helping Build the Economy

Let's take another trip to ancient Egypt, this time to a workshop filled with the clattering sounds of artisans. Here, too, women were present. They contributed their skills as craftswomen, their hands expertly crafting pottery or weaving intricate fabrics. Women also engaged in larger-scale production, intertwining their contributions into the very fabric of Egypt's booming economy. Their participation even here—not just as contributors but as essential components of its growth—shows how deeply women were embedded in the economic life of their society.

Barriers Abroad

Now, let's hit pause and compare this with the position of women in ancient Greece and Rome. There, women faced a whole bunch of legal and societal red tape. Greek women, for instance, could not own property independently and needed a male guardian's approval to participate in anything that involved money. Roman women, despite having some rights, still had the hassle of having to deal with a predominantly patriarchal structure. In contrast, Egyptian women, although still living in a male-dominated society, had the pleasure of working within a system that allowed them to be the architects of their financial destiny, driving home a message of gender equity far ahead of its time.

Patriarchy for Who?

The comparison with other ancient societies from around the same time highlights Egyptian women's unique position. In Mesopotamia, while women had certain rights, these were often overshadowed by laws protecting male superiority, something we know thanks to historical records (O'Brien, 1999). Meanwhile, in regions like ancient China, women's roles were predominantly determined by the patriarchy, so their public and economic interactions were limited. Against this backdrop, the rights and freedoms of Egyptian women set them apart, showcasing how much their civilization valued gender equality—at least when it came to the economy.

This freedom was a double-edged sword because it offered both opportunities and challenges. While women could steer their financial futures, societal expectations still shaped their experiences. Some women might have faced some backlash when exercising their rights, particularly those who dared to push beyond traditional boundaries (we'll learn all about them in the chapters to come). Despite this, the legal recognition of their rights was a powerful testament to their independence within ancient Egyptian culture.

House and Home

In the grand tapestry of ancient Egypt, where farmers toiled the earth and wooden boats floated along the Nile, women held significant power within their households. You may have guessed it from everything we've seen already, but Egyptian women weren't just bystanders but central figures in nurturing family dynamics and ensuring the continuity of their lineage.

Social Standing

So, we find ourselves in an ancient Egyptian home with vibrant colors splashed across the walls. Here, the woman of the house took being a homemaker to the next level, as she was the architect of familial alliances. By managing household affairs, she indirectly influenced social and political networks. She was the puppet master in the background, pulling all the right strings to make sure her family achieved the social status they wanted. Whether hosting gatherings or overseeing servants, she was integral to creating stability. Every decision she made rippled through her family's socio-political standing.

Like a backstage crew member at a theater, her influence was often unseen but crucial for the show's success.

Teaching the Children

On a typical day, a mother would gather her children—a lively band of young ones with curious eyes wide open—as she embarked on her daily educational duties, teaching them the essence of cultural rituals and religious beliefs. She would narrate tales of gods and goddesses, embedding societal values deep into their young hearts. Through bedtime stories under the starlit skies and songs sung by the River Nile, she ensured that the essence of Egyptian culture flowed uninterrupted from one generation to the next.

Mediating Marriages

But let's not forget the delicate dance of negotiating their children's marriages. This was a stage production where women took on roles akin to diplomats. They would spend hours hosting discussions revolving around the unions of their sons and daughters. This customary practice was as much about finding suitable partners for their children as it was a strategic game of chess that women played adeptly to forge powerful alliances. These negotiations often dictated the rise and fall of family fortunes through dowries and marriage contracts, and they added another layer to the intricate social hierarchy.

Helping Each Other Out

Beyond their immediate families, women acted as the glue binding broader community ties. They offered support during times of need, whether in the form of guidance on child-rearing or assistance during illness. It was like the ancient version of a group chat where the members helped each other out and offered advice. In this interconnected web, women visited one another's homes, shared resources, and engaged in communal activities. Through this, they strengthened social bonds and developed a collective resilience against life's adversities, cultivating a nurturing network within their neighborhoods.

The undeniable truth is that women in ancient Egypt held pivotal roles in both private and public spheres. Their ability to manage their households went so much further than just domestic work—it was a mastery of diplomacy and education that was vital for maintaining societal balance and harmony. Each lesson taught and each negotiation struck wove a legacy of strength and unity that has echoed through the ages.

So, let's tip our hats to these amazing women who, while often remaining in the shadows of history, commanded the torchlight that illuminated future generations. In understanding their lives, we discover inspiring role models whose legacies reflect empowerment, resilience, and a natural talent for leadership, resonating deeply with modern aspirations.

Women in Every Role

In the world of ancient Egypt, women defied expectations, proving themselves in a variety of professional fields. Their contributions were not only crucial to society at the time but still continue to serve as inspiring stories of historical figures who challenged societal norms. Let's look at a few of the professional roles that women played in ancient Egypt:

Scribes

One such role was that of the scribe. Literacy opened doors to many opportunities, and although it required years of study, dedicated women from families with members already in the field often pursued this path. As part of their duties, they managed records and administrative tasks and sometimes transitioned into prestigious positions like teaching or working within the priesthood.

Doctors and Healers

Women in ancient Egypt also made notable strides in the field of medicine. Female doctors and healers were highly esteemed, and some even attended Alexandria's renowned medical school. They developed treatments and even performed surgeries, leaving a lasting impact on the health care practices of the time.

Let's look at an example of one such extraordinary figure. Peseshet is recognized as one of the earliest known female physicians in history. She practiced medicine in around 2500 B.C.E., when women were often marginalized even in Egypt, as in many neighboring ancient societies. Nevertheless, her title, "The Lady Overseer of the Lady Physicians," suggests that she held a position of respect and responsibility.

There is evidence suggesting that she might have specialized in gynecology (Hurwitz, 2005). This area of medicine is vital, as it addresses women's health issues, which are often overlooked in historical contexts. If Peseshet had indeed focused on women's health, she would have been essential in providing care during pregnancy and childbirth as well as for other female-specific conditions. Her expertise would have undoubtedly encouraged trust and reliance among women in her community.

Today, the story of Peseshet can serve as motivation for you if you're an aspiring medical professional. It is a reminder that medicine is a field where both men and women can excel and make impactful contributions. Women continue to play significant roles in the medical field, often challenging the stereotypes and barriers that still exist. By celebrating figures like Peseshet, we can inspire the next generation of female health care professionals.

Artisans

Women artisans skillfully combined spiritual symbolism with craftsmanship, enriching Egypt's cultural legacy. They created intricate jewelry, textiles, and pottery, all of which were often linked to religious and ceremonial uses. This fusion of art and spirituality reflected their technical skills while also highlighting the significance of their contributions to the culture and religious expression of ancient Egypt.

Positions of Power

Social class influenced the professional opportunities available to Egyptian women. Those of higher status had access to education and could occupy roles such as priestesses or overseers within large households. Merneith, an early queen regent and possibly the first female pharaoh of Egypt, exemplifies how noble lineage let women wield significant power, sometimes even allowing them to function as rulers, even if they didn't carry the relevant titles. Lower-status women, on the other hand, typically found themselves in labor-intensive jobs or domestic roles. Regardless of their social standing, and as we discussed earlier, women maintained influence within their families and communities.

Brewers and Launderers

Female brewers and launderers often supervised male workers, showcasing their leadership and organizational skills even in more conventional settings. Their ability to navigate and manage these environments speaks to the broader sphere where women exerted control, further challenging what has commonly been assumed about gender roles in ancient societies.

The presence of women in these varied professions was a testament to their resilience and adaptability. While patriarchy heavily defined the external structures of society, women continuously carved out spaces of authority and autonomy. Their lives show us a different version of history than the one we're used to. It's an inspiring story of empowerment and self-determination that will no doubt resonate with you, hopefully encouraging you to pursue your aspirations irrespective of societal constraints.

Maybe you're wondering why it's important to examine these historical accounts. Well, it's so that we can draw parallels to contemporary discussions about gender equality and representation. The stories of these pioneering women reflect the timeless struggle for recognition and respect in professional spheres, and they can motivate you and the rest of your generation to continue advocating for equity and opportunity across all fields.

A Day in the Life

For women of this era, life was a tapestry woven with unique experiences, challenges, and triumphs. Personal accounts from historical texts offer us remarkable glimpses into these everyday realities, enriching our understanding and bringing us closer to these extraordinary women.

The Local Baker

In the scrolls and inscriptions that have survived thousands of years, we find stories of women juggling domestic responsibilities alongside community duties. Take, for instance, the tale of Maia, a woman who was responsible for baking bread not just for her family but for local festivals, too. Her hands were always busy kneading dough or carrying baskets of grain, painting a picture of diligence and dedication. Through examples like hers, we learn about the labors and tasks that filled a woman's day, allowing us to appreciate the strength required to manage the diverse roles she occupied.

The Priestess

These narratives also reveal the significant roles women held in spiritual and communal ceremonies. The echoes of ceremonial drums and chants serve as reminders of how vital women were in maintaining religious and cultural continuity. For example, let's talk about the great festival of Opet, a dramatic spectacle where women led the procession, their voices ringing with hymns as they engaged in ritual dances meant to honor the gods and ensure the prosperity of the land. Women like Meritamen, a priestess whose leadership in these celebrations underscored her cultural importance, captured the hearts and respect of those around her. Her influence was felt far beyond temple walls, resonating throughout the community.

The Businesswoman

The theme of resilience shines brightly in the stories of women who defied adversity with unyielding spirits. It's difficult not to feel admiration for women like Hemetre, who faced the trials of widowhood and managed her late husband's businesses. Although she encountered obstacles ranging from financial strains to assumptions about her capability, Hemetre's tenacity and determination to succeed became a beacon for her peers. In every challenge she conquered, there's a lesson in perseverance, reminding us that endurance can weave hope even in the bleakest times.

These personal stories resonate through time, imprinting a legacy that has shaped many generations. Women's lives were entwined with tales of survival, courage, and unwavering spirit, an inheritance passed down like heirloom necklaces from grandmother to granddaughter. They didn't merely exist in the shadow of men; they thrived and influenced the world around them. Their legacies were kept alive through oral traditions, familial teachings, and cultural practices. And so, the wisdom we've gained from their experiences remains embedded in our social fabric, influencing our movements and inspiring strength long after their physical presence has faded.

Be Inspired

For us today, these glimpses into women's lives in ancient Egypt offer guidance and encouragement. They remind us that despite different circumstances and being separated by millennia, human resilience and adaptability are timeless themes. As a young woman embarking on your own journey through school or the start of your career, you can draw parallels between your challenges and those faced by the women we encountered in this chapter, who balanced their personal aspirations with collective needs. You can be inspired by the empowerment and possibility they represent.

Explore further, and you'll discover that the narratives of this time are rich with inspiration for anyone striving to make an impact in their own world. They invite you to step into the sandals of those who came before you, who walked paths paved by strength, wisdom, and ambition. You'll see that, throughout history, women have always found ways to assert their autonomy and celebrate their identities, even when societal norms attempted to force them into a box. It's a potent reminder of the power you hold to carve out your niche, regardless of constraints imposed by time or tradition.

Conclusion

As we wrap up this fascinating journey through ancient Egypt's social landscape, it's clear that the women of this era were nothing short of remarkable. They ran households, managed properties, and deftly balanced family dynamics with the grace of a circus performer juggling flaming batons. These women weren't just sitting around in dusty old houses (or should we say mudbrick manors?). They were out there, hustling in marketplaces, crafting intricate jewelry, and even writing under flickering candlelight—much like you might when you're pulling an all-nighter before finals. Ancient Egyptian women managed to create their own brand of magic within society, seizing opportunities left, right, and center while probably inventing multitasking on the way.

Modern women have much in common with these ancient trailblazers, who remind us that we can tackle life's challenges head-on. Overcoming obstacles back then was as crucial as it is now, whether it involved educating kids about the many gods and goddesses or calling the shots on household decisions. These stories are super relatable, offering us life hacks for navigating present-day hurdles with creativity and resilience. So, the next time you're faced with a mountain of homework or a tricky life decision, channel your inner Egyptian queen—they knew how to handle things, and you might just discover some timeless wisdom from millennia past!

Chapter 2:

Divine Influencers—Goddesses of Ancient Egypt

In the mystical world of ancient Egypt, goddesses roamed as freely in the hearts of every Egyptian as they did in legends. Their temples were buzzing centers of divine activity and pyramid gossip, with our leading lady Isis at the heart of it all. She wielded maternal power like a weaponized hug, harnessing a blend of nurturing love and leadership that could bring even the fiercest crocodile to tears. Her mastery over balance was such that she could manage the cosmos and still have time for a cup of tea with Horus, her son, subtly reminding him to wear his crown straight while saving the universe from utter chaos. She wasn't just playing house; she was running the spiritual senate, proving that her maternal touch was nothing short of magical.

In this chapter, we'll explore how Isis and her fellow goddesses shaped the cosmos and everyday life with a dash of enchantment. We'll be getting lessons in leadership from formidable women like Bastet, whose role as the ultimate domestic goddess is told through stories of cats lounging like Egyptian royalty, teaching us mere mortals the art of balancing ferocity with feline grace. Sekhmet's duality will show us just how far you can stretch a lion metaphor without snapping it. Combining warrior strength with healer vibes, she's a cocktail of mighty roars and soft lulls. And of course, we can't forget the galaxy of lesser-known goddesses whose everyday influence ticked like a cosmic clock, connecting ancient yarns of empowerment with today's buzzwords of equality and self-discovery. So, grab your hieroglyphic decoder because we're about to wander down the Nile and into the world of ancient Egyptian mythology.

Isis: Protector and Leader

Isis, the most revered goddess of ancient Egypt, is a quintessential symbol of maternal power and leadership. Her divine story and attributes continue to resonate today and can inspire you to embrace your multifaceted identity.

Lessons We Can Learn From Isis

Throughout Egyptian mythology, Isis stands out not only for her nurturing qualities but also for her unyielding strength, providing an empowering image of femininity combined with resilience.

The Power of Compassion

A cornerstone of Isis's legacy is her nurturing nature, which has been pivotal in fostering the idea that true strength is rooted in compassion. As a mother, she exemplifies this through her undying love and protection for her son, Horus. The ancient tales tell us how she hid in the marshes of the Nile Delta to safeguard him from danger until he was strong enough to claim his rightful place as king. This dedication depicts a profound sense of resilience, as Isis faced numerous challenges yet remained steadfast through them all. Today, these qualities serve as a reminder that nurturing doesn't equate to weakness; instead, it showcases the enormous power of empathy and care.

The Power to Overcome

Another aspect of Isis's mythology that highlights her influence on family and society is her pivotal role in the myth of Osiris, her husband. As it's told, Set, a trickster and sky god, betrayed Osiris and then dismembered him. Isis displayed unparalleled determination by gathering the pieces of his body, which had been scattered across Egypt. Employing her magical abilities, she resurrected her husband and conceived her son, ensuring the cycle of life continued and birthing a new era for Horus. This act symbolizes rebirth, demonstrating the importance of confronting adversity for growth—a powerful lesson when you're navigating personal and societal challenges. Essentially, overcoming them is about finding hope amid despair, just like how Isis found light in reviving Osiris.

The Power of Femininity

Isis's authority extends beyond her familial roles, challenging historical stereotypes about femininity and power. Unlike other deities depicted solely in domestic or nurturing roles, and reflecting the role of women in ancient Egypt, Isis held substantial influence over the spiritual and civic realms of the land. She was deeply revered as a protector, healer, and magician whose powers transcended even other deities. This multifaceted persona breaks conventional molds, promoting empathy and wisdom as integral components of leadership. Today, Isis symbolizes a harmonious balance between strength and compassion, encouraging you to challenge societal norms and embrace your diverse strengths in leadership roles.

The Power of Being Dynamic

When you examine modern representations of Isis, you will find a rich landscape of cultural empowerment connecting the past with the present. Today, Isis is an inspiration to approach your identity with openness and confidence. Like the goddess who embraced multiple roles—from nurturing mother to mighty protector—you, too, can pursue varied paths, whether in your education, career, or social advocacy. The flexibility and depth of Isis's character are a reminder that these roles do not confine you but rather enhance the richness of your experiences.

Modern Influence

We see echoes of Isis's influence in contemporary movements advocating for women's rights and gender equality. These initiatives often highlight the compatibility of strength and empathy, drawing from historical icons like Isis to validate their narratives. By embodying both maternal instincts and authoritative presence, women today can redefine leadership roles, resonating deeply with the ideals personified by this ancient goddess.

In creative arts and literature, Isis continues to inspire tales of feminine heroism and mystical adventures. Her stories transcend the boundaries of time, serving as a reminder that empowerment has long been an integral part of the female experience. Whether in ancient scripts or modern novels, Isis's legacy remains a beacon of hope for anyone exploring their place within history and culture.

From intricate statues in the Greco-Roman world to stunning temple reliefs in Egypt, her image, which has been a muse for expressions of grace intertwined with formidable might, has captivated artists for centuries. These portrayals serve as visual affirmations of her enduring relevance and appeal.

Modern interpretations of Isis can provide you with a framework for understanding the blend of past traditions and present ambitions. By embracing her spirit, you can navigate your own identity with confidence, much like Isis wielded her skills and intuition to shape the cosmos around her. This connection between history and modern values creates a powerful narrative where you might find inspiration to grow, lead, and inspire.

Bastet: The Guardian

In the bustling and colorful world of ancient Egyptian mythology, Bastet was a goddess who stood out with her harmonious blend of ferocity and warmth. Often portrayed as a domestic guardian, Bastet took on the vital role of protector and nurturer, ensuring happiness and safety within family dynamics. When coming home after a long day in ancient Egypt, it was believed that you would be greeted not just by your earthly family but also by the watchful eyes of the goddess herself. Her presence symbolized that true strength didn't lie only in fighting enemies but also in fostering an environment where families thrived in happiness and security.

The Divine Cat

Depictions of Bastet often featured cats, creatures that have long been associated with comfort and companionship. Even millennia ago, these creatures lounged around homes, quietly observing the world with a mysterious air—much like Bastet's own subtle yet significant influence on domestic life. In ancient Egypt, cats were not just cuddly companions. They were considered divine and reflections of Bastet's energy, teaching the Egyptians to respect and appreciate their four-legged friends. This reverence extended beyond the furry faces peeking out from behind pottery or basking in sunshine; it was a lesson about valuing the bonds and tranquility found within the sacred spaces of the home.

The Feasts of Bubastis

Take yourself back in time to around 2000 B.C.E. and imagine an Egyptian festival brimming with music, dancing, and laughter that echoed through the streets and all around the town. In the city, the Feast of Bubastis, a celebration honoring Bastet, was a community event where everyone was invited to partake. These joyous gatherings highlighted the incredible importance of togetherness and relationships, proving that the bonds you share can uplift and protect you as surely as any mighty goddess. While they were also about having fun, the festivities were testaments to how nurturing connections cultivated both personal and collective strength.

Modern Influence

Fast forward to today, and Bastet remains a symbol of empowerment. Modern interpretations of her legacy continue to prove that history shapes our understanding of domestic roles.

Redefining Domesticity

In contemporary culture, Bastet emerges as a muse who can empower you to redefine domesticity, just as she did. She challenged outdated stereotypes, portraying the home not as a place of confinement but as a realm of influence and leadership. Today, women draw strength from their home lives to effect change, echoing Bastet's timeless wisdom. You may have grown up seeing examples of this in the way your mother, aunts, or other strong women approached their households. Through fashion, social media, and art, Bastet has also inspired discussions on gender equality and balance, bridging the gap between past and present.

Finding Harmony

Modern fans of Bastet might download aesthetic wallpapers of feline images or scroll through social media feeds adorned with cat-motif jewelry, aligning these symbols with their femininity and quests for harmony in daily life (Long, 2023). Bastet makes cameo appearances in art, films, and even hashtags. Fictional tales where she is mentioned or depicted, like *Black Panther*, explore her mythology with a sense of wonder. Her celestial charm continues to inspire narratives that may speak to you as you navigate your identity, empowering you to create nurturing environments while possibly pursuing leadership roles or aiming to make a societal impact.

Bastet's continued influence reveals a dynamic relationship between ancient myth and modern identity. Her lasting appeal lies in her ability to stay eternally relevant, blending the ancient essence of protection and nurture with a contemporary message of empowerment and equality. It's no wonder she remains etched in our cultural consciousness, reminding us that each home can be a sanctuary of strength. Whether through art installations or cinematic works, Bastet's enduring presence offers a comforting nod of encouragement as you forge new paths, assuring you that you are watched over by a legacy of courage, loyalty, and love.

Sekhmet: The Goddess of War

Sekhmet's reputation as both a fierce protector and compassionate healer made her an extraordinary figure in ancient Egypt. Known as the goddess of war, Sekhmet's very essence inspired those who sought empowerment through justice. Beyond seeing her as a symbol of brute strength, her admirers also saw her as a testament to the fiery passion needed to pursue equality and fairness. Today, embracing Sekhmet's spirit means channeling your inner strength to rise up against injustice. The stories of her valor encourage you to spearhead changes in society with both courage and conviction.

The Healer

Sekhmet was more than just a warrior. As a healer, her presence brought comfort and relief to those in need. She was revered by physicians and associated with miraculous healing powers. This duality highlighted how leadership is not just defined by power but also by empathy and care for others. Her nurturing side reminds us that compassion is a powerful tool in any community. In our modern world, embodying these traits will allow you to create environments where people—whether your friends, family, or future colleagues—can thrive and support each other to become stronger together.

Collective Manifestation

Rituals and worship of Sekhmet played an important role in fostering communal bonds. These ceremonies were more than mere acts of tradition; they were pivotal moments when people contributed their energy and intentions toward collective growth and protection. These gatherings underscored the significance of each person's role in their society. By participating in these rituals, ancient Egyptians felt empowered and connected, laying the groundwork for unity and collaborative strength. This continues to resonate today, teaching us how social connectedness is strengthened through shared customs and mutual respect.

The Lioness

One of the most striking aspects of Sekhmet is her depiction as a lioness, a symbol packed with layers of meaning. Lions have long been admired for their power and majesty, yet in Sekhmet, this strength is combined with the gentleness of a healer. This complexity urges us to look beyond gender stereotypes, inviting a broader understanding of femininity. It suggests that as a woman, you can be strong without neglecting tenderness and that you can be assertive without losing your capacity for kindness. Even now, the lioness form of Sekhmet supports the idea that your identity is multifaceted and encourages you to accept all of the aspects of your nature—the fierce, the gentle, and everything in between.

Lesser-Known Goddesses

In ancient Egypt, the important roles goddesses played often intertwined with everyday life, offering empowerment and lessons that resonate even today. While Isis and Bastet are more familiar names, lesser-known goddesses like Hathor, Ma'at, and Neith also held significant influence in shaping societal values and personal beliefs.

Hathor

Hathor was a goddess deeply associated with love, beauty, music, dance, and fertility. She was the ultimate muse who spurred creativity and celebrated joy. However, her connection to the arts transcended entertainment; it was seen as a divine form of self-expression. In a world without modern distractions, music and dance were powerful tools for storytelling and conveying emotions. Music could comfort, unite communities, or alleviate the stressors of daily struggles.

Hathor's influence encouraged people to channel their struggles into creative outlets, emphasizing the transformative power of art. By tapping into these creative energies, people found ways to overcome personal hurdles and celebrate both triumphs and challenges through song and dance. For the ancient Egyptians, it was like that playlist you have that makes you feel invincible.

Ma'at

Ma'at was a goddess synonymous with truth, balance, and cosmic order. Her name itself became a term for the principle she embodied: the harmonious order that ensured the universe functioned smoothly. She was often depicted walking around ancient Egypt with her feather, weighing the hearts of those in the afterlife against it. A simple yet profound metaphor for justice, don't you think?

Ma'at wasn't just an esoteric ideal; she represented the moral backbone of society. Women, in particular, looked to Ma'at as a model of integrity who could show them how to play a vital role in upholding ethical norms. Her influence suggested that truth and justice were not only divine principles but also accessible and essential for everyday interactions. The embodiment of Ma'at emphasizes how women have always been naturally aligned with fairness and honesty, qualities crucial in maintaining the social fabric of their families and communities.

Neith

Neith embodied the duality of creation and destruction, crafting a narrative that embraced diverse skills and roles. As one of the earliest deities, she was known as both a creator goddess and a fearsome warrior. Think of her as part artist, part commander in chief, effortlessly balancing fierceness with creativity. Her duality offered a refreshing view on gender equality, affirming that strength and artistry can go hand in hand. Her tale is also a reminder that the interests you might perceive as opposites can coexist harmoniously. Today, Neith's versatility can teach you that being multifaceted is powerful, challenging the idea that you need to fit into a narrow role.

Rituals Performed to Honor These Goddesses

Exploring how the lesser-known goddesses were worshipped highlights women's involvement in religious and societal structures. In temples and in home life, women actively participated in rituals and ceremonies dedicated to deities. These practices were more than religious obligations; they were communal experiences that solidified women's positions in spiritual life.

Women served as priestesses in charge of leading prayers and guiding spiritual journeys. The rituals they oversaw were the core of community life. They fostered unity and provided a sense of purpose, and their involvement equipped women with a space where they could exert influence and leadership. In this way, we can see how ancient beliefs and practices connect with modern ideas of empowerment.

Women's active participation in worship reflects an early form of societal leadership that resonates with the current pursuit of gender equality. By learning from these historical figures, especially as you're navigating your identity, you can draw parallels with your own life. The roles the goddesses occupied remind us that the intersection of creativity, justice, multifaceted abilities, and spiritual engagement can be a starting point for empowerment and growth.

Conclusion

As we've continued our journey through the mystical land of ancient Egypt, we've met an impressive lineup of deities who definitely knew how to own the stage. First up was the ever-inspiring Isis, who's basically the Beyoncé of goddesses. With her nurturing heart and epic determination, she seamlessly combined empathy with a flair for leadership—talk about multitasking! Her story is a reminder that being strong doesn't mean you can't show a little love and compassion along the way. Fast forward to today, and Isis is still whispering encouragement to young women everywhere, urging them to juggle roles like a pro while breaking down barriers faster than you can say "Horus."

Meanwhile, Bastet's not-so-secret superpower was making home life feel as cozy as that perfect pair of fuzzy socks. As the ultimate guardian—and with a thing for cats—she taught the Egyptians that true power involves bringing happiness and security into family life, which means binge-watching cat videos might have roots stretching back thousands of years. Sekhmet, with her lioness swagger, is proof that you can be a fierce battle fiend and a tender healer, leaving a legacy that's more layered than your grandma's lasagna. Each goddess, with her unique flair, basks in the spotlight of history, showing you that strength takes many forms—from dance moves at a festival honoring Bastet to Sekhmet's ferocious yet gentle roar. So, keep these lessons close as you continue crafting your own life of empowerment.

Chapter 3:

Ruling Beyond Gender—The Female Pharaohs

When it comes to ruling beyond gender, the story of female pharaohs in ancient Egypt is like a plot twist that makes you sit up and say, "Wait, what?" It was a time when only men could claim the throne, and yet there they were—women stepping up to the plate with all the grace of a feline stalking through reeds. These trailblazing queens did so much more than take on the crown: They redefined what it meant to wear it.

This chapter unravels the tales of these extraordinary icons who turned societal norms upside down while tossing in some seriously impressive architectural wonders and trade routes for good measure. Their reigns were not just about proving a point but showing how strength and strategy can transcend traditional roles. Through them, we get a glimpse into a world where leadership was defined by power and influence, not gender.

Brace yourself for legendary tales about groundbreaking rulers like Hatshepsut, Sobekneferu, Nefertiti, and Cleopatra VII. These women weren't content with being footnotes in history; they took center stage and owned it. From Hatshepsut's commanding mortuary temple at Deir el-Bahari to Sobekneferu's unforgettable architectural legacies, each pharaoh brought their own flair to governance.

Get ready to learn all about Nefertiti's coregency and religious reforms during the Amarna Period, where she played both political chess and spiritual leader. Meanwhile, you'll discover how Cleopatra VII dazzled and outmaneuvered her way through Roman alliances like a master strategist in a high-stakes game of Risk. More than simply recounting past achievements, this chapter is an opportunity to understand how these powerful women navigated and transformed their worlds, leaving behind enduring marks that continue to inspire and challenge perceptions of leadership to this day.

Sobekneferu

Amid the sands of ancient Egypt stood a trailblazer whose name is often whispered with awe: Sobekneferu. It was around 1806 B.C.E., and the Egyptian throne sat empty following the death of Pharaoh Amenemhet IV. Enter Sobekneferu, daughter of Amenemhat III, who stepped forward to claim her rightful place.

Ruling during the 12th Dynasty, she came into power in an era where female rulers were as rare as a cool breeze in the desert. The idea of a female pharaoh was revolutionary at the time, especially in such a powerful civilization. But Sobekneferu was not just any young woman. She was a pioneer who challenged the status quo, showcasing the potential for female leadership even in the most patriarchal societies.

Sobekneferu's reign, despite lasting just under four years, was marked by extraordinary achievements that carved her name into history as one of the earliest known female pharaohs, one who defied the customs of her time and wielded power in a male-dominated world.

Redefining Power

One of the most notable aspects of Sobekneferu's reign was her strategic approach to her presentation. While she embraced her female identity, she donned the traditional garb of a male pharaoh. Her statues depicted her in full royal regalia, adorned with symbols of masculinity traditionally reserved for men. By presenting herself as a formidable leader despite being a woman, this bold move allowed her to navigate the intricate gender expectations of the time with finesse. In this way, Sobekneferu challenged social norms and redefined what it meant to be a ruler—a testament to her resilience and ingenuity.

The Innovative Architect

Sobekneferu wasn't just about appearances. She also left her mark on the landscape of Egypt itself, commissioning significant projects and leaving behind a legacy of grandeur that spoke volumes of her commitment to public works and cultural development. One noteworthy example was her work on the labyrinth at Amenemhet III's funerary complex in Hawara, a marvel of engineering that displayed her dedication to honoring her predecessors and advancing architectural innovation. She also enhanced Shedet, the religious center in Crocodilopolis that honored the crocodile god Sobek, her namesake. Through these projects, she etched her influence into the very stones of Egypt, ensuring that her vision would echo through time.

Sobekneferu's architectural contributions reflected her ambition and leadership skills. Her projects were as much about establishing her authority and leaving a lasting mark on Egypt's history as they were about aesthetics. By studying her constructions, we gain insights into how Sobekneferu used architecture as a tool for both governance and cultural expression.

Sobekneferu's Legacy

Although she sat on the throne for only a brief period—from 1806 to 1802 B.C.E.—Sobekneferu's impact transcended her lifetime. Her reign ended the prosperous Middle Kingdom, yet her influence endured, paving the way for future female leaders like Hatshepsut and Cleopatra. By proving that leadership was not limited by gender, Sobekneferu has inspired women throughout history to challenge societal constraints and pursue positions of power.

In the broader context of female empowerment and leadership, her legacy serves as a guiding light. She embodied courage, determination, and adaptability, facing resistance with unwavering resolve. Her story resonates today, and she serves as a role model who exemplifies strength and resilience in breaking down gender barriers. Her life and reign offer valuable lessons on navigating challenges, asserting identity, and leaving an unforgettable legacy.

The importance of Sobekneferu's reign lies not only in her achievements but also in the doors she opened for future generations. As the first confirmed female pharaoh, she set the standard for female leadership in ancient Egypt, challenging deeply entrenched norms and redefining what it meant to rule. Her story is a testament to the enduring struggle for gender equality. Her triumphs and trials remind us that it is often those brave enough to challenge convention and imagine new possibilities who forge progress.

Sobekneferu's story stands out as a beacon of empowerment and transformation. Her contributions and legacy serve as a road map for aspiring leaders eager to leave their mark on the world. Through her example, we learn that true leadership knows no gender, and we are inspired to envision a world where anyone can rise to greatness, leaving a blazing trail for others to follow.

Hatshepsut

Hatshepsut, one of ancient Egypt's most remarkable female pharaohs, was a master at using symbolism and political maneuvering to legitimize her reign. At a time when women were rarely seen as rulers, her rise to power was nothing short of revolutionary. Her story is an inspiring tale of courage and ingenuity, demonstrating how she cleverly navigated her way through a male-dominated society.

Making a Statement

Imagine being in Hatshepsut's shoes, the daughter of a pharaoh who'd died with no sons, surrounded by the belief that only men could rule as kings and constrained by a system where only sons could inherit the throne. Still, she didn't sit back and accept the status quo. She took charge, marrying her half-brother to secure him the throne. Later, after her husband's death and once she'd claimed the seat of power, she commissioned grand structures that would stand as timeless testaments to her strength and vision.

Among her most significant achievements is the mortuary temple nestled against the cliffs at Deir el-Bahari. This architectural marvel was not just a place for her afterlife; it was a bold statement asserting her right to the throne. The temple, with its impressive terraces and colonnades, has been hailed as one of ancient Egypt's greatest architectural feats (*Hatshepsut: History of Architecture*, 2024). But Hatshepsut knew that monuments alone wouldn't suffice to cement her power. She understood the importance of titles and names in shaping identity and perception. So, what did she do?

She adopted titles traditionally reserved for male pharaohs. By following Sobekneferu's lead and presenting herself as both king and queen—for example, wearing the clothing of a male pharaoh, fake beard included—she reshaped the narrative around female leadership, challenging the patriarchal norms that dominated Egyptian society. Her strategic use of male attributes in art and inscriptions helped establish her authority in the eyes of her subjects.

The Savvy Economist

Hatshepsut revitalized Egypt's trade networks, understanding that economic prowess was the cornerstone of strong leadership. One of her most celebrated ventures was the expedition to Punt (an ancient country in Africa), a land rich in treasures like gold, ivory, and exotic incense. This journey was a strategic move to showcase Egypt's wealth and influence under her rule (PBS, 2020). The successful mission bolstered her image as a capable and prosperous leader, reminding everyone that she was more than fit to wear the crown.

The Power of Perception

To weave her story into the cultural fabric, Hatshepsut also turned to propaganda and art. Imagery and narratives were powerful tools, and she used them expertly to convey her legitimacy and achievements. On the walls of her temple, she depicted divine birth stories that linked her directly to the gods, reinforcing her right to rule. Portraying herself with male traits in statues and carvings, another measure she took, was about crafting the narrative that she was worthy of respect and recognition.

What We Can Learn

Here's how you can use her strategies today: Use all the resources available to you to craft a compelling narrative. Whether you're trying to change how people see you or establish credibility, leveraging storytelling—through art, fashion, words, or actions—is essential. Like Hatshepsut, who used her temple walls as a canvas to illustrate her godly heritage, you can use the platforms available to you, like social media, to shape your narrative and influence public perception.

While monumental architecture and trade expeditions might seem distant from our current reality, the essence of Hatshepsut's tactics is eminently relatable. She exemplifies how determination and strategy can overcome societal barriers, offering invaluable lessons on leadership. Her story is a saga of empowerment. It's about embracing your unique strengths and abilities, even when the odds seem stacked against you.

Nefertiti

Nefertiti, the iconic queen of ancient Egypt, stands out as a remarkable figure within the pages of history. Her reign alongside Pharaoh Akhenaten during the Amarna Period marked an era of profound religious and cultural transformation. By stepping into a role traditionally dominated by men, Nefertiti challenged gender norms and held considerable political power, forever changing perceptions of what it meant to be queen in ancient times.

A New Type of Queen

Beyond being a marital alliance, the partnership between Nefertiti and Akhenaten extended deeply into the sphere of governance. Unlike many queens before her, Nefertiti exerted significant authority and served as her husband's equal. This dynamic allowed her to support Akhenaten's visions while also actively participating in making them a reality. It was through this unique relationship that traditional views of female authority were tested and reshaped, showcasing how power dynamics could be renegotiated regardless of societal conventions.

A New God

One of Nefertiti's most notable influences was her central role in the establishment of a new religious order centered around Aten, the sun disk. Previously, Egyptian religious practices revolved around a complex pantheon of gods, with Amun, the god of the air, being at the forefront. However, under Akhenaten's rule, there was a radical shift toward worshipping Aten as the singular deity. The queen's involvement in this transition was pivotal, positioning her as a religious leader as well as a key architect in reshaping spiritual expression. She is often depicted in art performing rituals associated with Atenism. More than mere symbolism, this was a reflection of her active engagement in redefining the empire's divine focus and suggests that she had a level of autonomy unprecedented for a queen (History.com Editors, 2019).

A New Kind of Power

Artistic representations of Nefertiti, in which she is famously portrayed wearing her distinctive flat-topped crown, further underscore her influential status. These depictions served both as a testament to her influence and a statement on the perception of women in power. Unlike earlier representations of queens, which often highlighted passive roles or secondary positions, Nefertiti is frequently shown engaging in actions reserved for pharaohs. Icons of her smiting enemies or leading religious ceremonies articulate a narrative where beauty and authority coexist harmoniously. This artistry played an important part in cementing her legacy, extending her influence far beyond the confines of her era.

Still, Nefertiti's path to power was not devoid of challenges. Navigating the political landscape of ancient Egypt required strategic wisdom, especially in light of opposition from those resistant to change. Despite these difficulties, she managed to maintain her position and continue her influence, demonstrating a level of tenacity that you can take inspiration from. Her ability to persevere amid adversity offers invaluable lessons in leadership, driving home the importance of being resilient when you are faced with obstacles.

Cleopatra VII

Both revered and reviled, Cleopatra VII reigns as one of history's most intriguing figures. Born into an Egyptian dynasty of Greek origin, Cleopatra dared to defy conventions in a kingdom rife with political instability. Let's explore how she navigated through the stormy tides of power, her alliances with Roman leaders, confrontations with gender bias, and the legacy she forged.

A Woman of the People

Cleopatra's era was characterized by a turbulent political landscape, not unlike the shifting sands of power we see today. Her rule began under a cloud of familial discord with her brother Ptolemy XIII, who banished her. The internal conflicts within the royal family were coupled with external threats from a burgeoning Roman Empire eager for control over Egyptian riches. Still, Cleopatra showed extraordinary political awareness in the face of these challenges. She took decisive steps, like learning the native Egyptian language rather than adhering strictly to her Macedonian roots. This seemingly small act elevated her status among her subjects, distinguishing her from previous rulers who hadn't bothered to connect so directly with the people they governed.

A Powerful Alliance

One of Cleopatra's most notable maneuvers was her strategic alignment with Rome's most prominent men. When Julius Caesar arrived in ancient Egypt's capital, Alexandria, amid his campaign against Pompey the Great, a fellow Roman, Cleopatra saw an opportunity. With characteristic flair, she famously smuggled herself into his quarters, a bold entrance that caught Caesar's attention and respect. Despite their different backgrounds, the two formed a powerful alliance, one marked by mutual interests and a romantic connection. Their relationship is what enabled Cleopatra to reclaim her throne after being ousted by her brother.

Following Caesar's assassination, Cleopatra's diplomatic dance continued with Mark Antony, another powerful Roman figure. This union showcased her deep understanding of Roman politics and her ability to maintain Egypt's autonomy. Antony and Cleopatra's partnership was as much political as it was personal, each viewing the other as vital to their respective goals. Together, they sought to consolidate power and resist Octavian, Julius Caesar's heir. Despite their eventual defeat at the Battle of Actium, their story has been immortalized through history and art, showing how Cleopatra embodied both romantic and imperial ambitions.

Misrepresented and Misunderstood

Cleopatra's political engagements also highlighted the pervasive gender biases of her time. As a woman who held considerable influence, the skepticism she faced during her reign has continued throughout history. Her intelligence and charisma often got overshadowed by narratives focusing on her beauty or romantic liaisons. Such portrayals have persisted into the modern era, revealing ongoing struggles against stereotypical depictions of women leaders. The ancient accounts that painted her as manipulative or immorally seductive often served the purposes of her male adversaries, who sought to diminish her achievements in governance and diplomacy.

Despite the struggles, Cleopatra's enduring conviction shines through. Though ultimately overtaken by Roman forces led by Octavian—who would become Emperor Augustus—how she was defeated speaks volumes about her character. Faced with inevitable capture and humiliation, she chose control over her fate, reputedly ending her life by allowing an asp, a venomous snake, to bite her. This decision has resounded through the ages, symbolizing her defiance and agency even in death.

Cleopatra's Legacy

Cleopatra's legacy is one of intriguing contradiction. On the one hand, she is remembered as a captivating and controversial figure; on the other, she is celebrated as a queen whose leadership skills ensured Egypt's independence for a time. Her legacy teaches us about the complexities of leadership, especially for women navigating patriarchal structures. Her life illustrates the power dynamics that have persisted across centuries, where women in power must continually strategize to assert their place within hierarchies traditionally dominated by men.

Her story invites comparisons to current discussions about gender equality and leadership. As a role model who embodies strength and inner power, Cleopatra stands as a testament to the potential of young women to challenge norms and craft influential legacies. She is a reminder that setbacks do not diminish your impact. Rather, being knocked down can fortify your resolve and help you inspire others to strive for resilience in the face of adversity.

Conclusion

From the sands of Egypt rises a tale as timeless as the pyramids, one filled with drama and sheer tenacity. Hatshepsut, who rocked the pharaoh scene like an ancient Taylor Swift, made her grand mark with stone masterpieces and trade conquests. Her story is a wild ride of flipping gender rules on their ancient heads, proving that you can rule fiercely no matter what anyone thinks! Like her, you can channel your inner architect—because why wouldn't you want to design something epic when you're reshaping history? Her mastery of storytelling through monuments shows us that self-expression has always been chic, solidifying her spot in history as a leader who knew that the power of presentation was everything.

But let's not forget Sobekneferu, trailblazing through history like the ultimate boss queen. Though her reign sparked like a short-lived firework, it lit up new ideals of female leadership way before hashtags were a thing. Imagine stepping onto a throne amid swirling political winds, wearing symbols borrowed from men yet standing firm as an icon of women's potential. She built her legacy with grand structures, leaving behind sites that whispered her name long after she was gone. It's a reminder that sometimes the impact isn't measured by length but by the depth of change sparked. And for anyone facing their own deserts of doubt, her courage runs parallel, encouraging us all to embrace strength even when the journey gets turbulent.

Chapter 4:

Queens at the Helm—Power Beyond the Throne

When you step into the realm of queens and royal women, you'll find a world of political finesse, diplomatic maneuvering, and a few unexpected twists. Forget everything you thought you knew about ancient Egypt being ruled solely by pharaohs lounging around with their crooks and flails. Instead, picture a chessboard where queens were often the key to victory, with Tiye playing one of the most compelling games of her time. Not satisfied with just smiling and waving next to Amenhotep III, she artfully juggled alliances and treaties, quelling potential conflicts long before they became headlines, or should we say, hieroglyphs on temple walls?

In this next stage of our journey, we plunge into the lives and legacies of these regal powerhouses. From Tiye's savvy diplomacy and strategic marriages that fortified the whole kingdom to the monumental influence Nefertari wielded through architecture and spiritual endeavors, this chapter is packed with fascinating stories about game-changing moves. We'll explore how Ankhesenamun's daring political strategies rival any modern-day thriller, see the complexities behind royal unions, and witness the indelible marks these resilient rulers have left on history. Prepare for a whirlwind expedition where traditional roles blur, authority transcends gender, and the sands of time are etched with tales of enduring determination.

Queen Tiye

The story of Queen Tiye stands as a testament to the power and influence women wielded from behind the throne. As a queen who lived during Egypt's 18th Dynasty, around 1398–1338 B.C.E., Tiye's diplomatic prowess was nothing short of legendary. In addition to supporting her husband, Pharaoh Amenhotep III, she also played an instrumental role in shaping Egypt's foreign policy and navigating international relations.

The Diplomat

Tiye was not just a figurehead; she was an active participant in steering the nation's affairs. Her most significant contribution was her role as an intermediary in treaties and alliances, through which her involvement was crucial in maintaining peace and stability. Imagine ancient Egypt at the center of a chessboard where the nation was at stake, each move needing to be carefully planned to keep the kingdom secure. Tiye managed these complex interactions with finesse. Think of her as the grand master, sitting in meetings with scribes and advisors, reviewing proposals from neighboring rulers and considering their implications on the political landscape. The wealth accumulated through trade, gifts, and mutual defense pacts formed during her time contributed significantly to the internal stability and economic strength of the kingdom.

Her direct communication with foreign leaders is another intriguing aspect of her diplomatic influence. Unlike many of her contemporaries who relied solely on representatives or third parties, Tiye often communicated directly with powerful figures from other countries. This unmediated engagement demonstrated her intelligence and authority. Her letters likely showcased her eloquence, and her carefully crafted messages were seemingly persuasive enough to sway other rulers and kings. Such correspondences helped in forming strategic alliances and perhaps even cooled tensions that might have arisen due to territorial disputes or resource shortages.

A Strategic Alliance

Now, let's talk about her marriage to Amenhotep III, which was far more than a union based on romance. It was a partnership fundamentally rooted in strategy. Although she married into one of the most powerful dynasties, Tiye, who was the daughter of an official and not royal by blood, brought considerable wealth and political clout to the relationship. Upon entering the king's court, she was a woman whose family connections strengthened Amenhotep's reign. Their combined influence ensured that Egypt remained prosperous and secured its position as a major power player in the ancient world.

Tiye's Legacy

Beyond her immediate actions, Tiye's legacy offers inspiration to generations of women. She exemplified how female influence could alter political landscapes. Hers isn't simply a tale of the past—it's a story that resonates today. In Tiye, you can see a role model who defied the expectations of her era. Her story affirms that historical figures of great influence weren't confined to traditional roles; they had the strength to step beyond their imposed limitations and shape the course of events.

Tiye's life provides guidelines for standing firm and negotiating formidable paths despite restrictive circumstances. Her mastery in crafting alliances and engaging directly with powerful leaders serves as a blueprint as you navigate modern complexities, especially in leadership and, maybe one day, politics. Whether you're discussing new student council policies or negotiating cheer team dynamics, the essence of Tiye's impact—understanding when to communicate directly and how to build effective partnerships—will prove relevant in its timelessness.

Queen Nefertari

Nefertari, the treasured Great Royal Wife of Ramses II, did more than stand beside him as his queen. She also left an unforgettable mark on Egypt through her influence on monumental architecture, a testament to her power, intellect, and spiritual eminence. Her legacy is carved into the rocks of Abu Simbel, where, at first glance, Nefertari's temple, built in her honor by her husband, may appear to be just another example of ancient Egyptian grandeur. However, every inch is filled with symbolism and cultural narratives that illuminate her significant role in shaping history.

Nefertari's Temple

Let's start by appreciating the significance of having a temple named after you in ancient Egypt. Nefertari's temple at Abu Simbel stands alongside the grand temple of Ramses II, placing her importance on par with the pharaoh himself and asserting her place in the cosmic order and society. This physical proximity to the king in monumental architecture says much about her elevated status and influence during their rule. Unlike many queens who were often overshadowed by their royal husbands, Nefertari was celebrated in life and immortalized in stone. This is a clear sign of her remarkable standing within the kingdom.

Nefertari's representation in the temple's art offers a window into her dynamic roles as a queen and mother. These images, while beautifying the space, also hold stories of her strength and divinity. The walls are adorned with rich artistic depictions illustrating her participation in various ceremonial rituals. There she stands, dressed in flowing regalia, sometimes even shown interacting with gods—especially Hathor, the goddess of motherhood, joy, and music. Through these portrayals, we witness an embodiment of grace and authority, a woman whose powers transcended her earthly presence. She is shown not only as a nurturing figure but as a woman with divine connections, bridging the world of gods and humans with elegance and intelligence.

Mistress of Upper and Lower Egypt

We cannot explore Nefertari's architectural influence without considering her religious endeavors, which were equally significant. In ancient Egypt, religion was intertwined with governance and daily life. Nefertari's active involvement in religious activities demonstrated her spiritual prowess and reinforced the acceptance of female authority in sacred matters. According to records, she played a significant role in ceremonial events, including those dedicated to deities like Hathor and Isis (History Skills, n.d.). Her title, "Mistress of Upper and Lower Egypt," speaks volumes about her acknowledged wisdom and spirituality. This reinforced the reverence for women in religious hierarchies, allowing them to operate as spiritual guides within society.

Women Shaping History

Nefertari's contributions showcase how women's leadership has shaped cultural legacies throughout history. By commissioning grand projects and participating actively in state and religious affairs, she set a precedent for future generations. Her actions served as blueprints for other royal women who followed in her footsteps and asserted their power in matters of statecraft and spiritual expression. Her story illustrates a counter-narrative to the often male-dominated historical accounts, offering inspiration and empowerment to women today. As she was a powerful figure whose contributions went beyond traditional roles, you might find a reflection of your aspirations in her example.

When it comes to the notion of female spiritual authority, Nefertari utilized her position to influence the public perception of women in leadership. Not content with mere ceremonial involvement, she engaged with prominent figures and participated in decisions that affected Egyptian society and its relationship with neighboring regions. Her strategic placements of temples and participation in religious ceremonies were forms of soft diplomacy that ensured that alliances were maintained and that Egypt's interests were safeguarded.

Nefertari's Legacy

In terms of her legacy, Nefertari's lasting impact can be measured through the reactions and respect she has garnered from subsequent generations. Her ability to affect change and embody power beyond the throne did not fade with her death; it has continued throughout history, offering lessons in diplomacy, governance, and spirituality. The dreams she etched in stone have resonated across millennia and into today, inspiring and encouraging us to pursue our dreams with vigor and resilience.

It's through this lens that we should appreciate Nefertari's architectural ambitions. We see that they were not merely expressions of aesthetic prowess but statements of power and reform. Her story proclaims that true influence is not bound by gender or tradition. You might even envision her as a relatable figure who wielded her influence thoughtfully and effectively, paving paths where there once were none.

Ankhesenamun

We've already covered that ancient Egypt was a land of gods, pharaohs, and pyramids. But it also came with some pretty intense family drama. Now, enter Ankhesenamun, born Ankhesenaten, a queen whose agility in political maneuvering was as captivating as the hieroglyphics that recorded her past. Her life might sound like it came straight out of an Egyptian soap opera, but trust me, it's all facts.

The Backstory

Ankhesenamun was born into the house of Pharaoh Akhenaten and Queen Nefertiti, who you might recall from Chapter 3. These two had turned the traditional religious order on its head by championing Aten, the sun disk, over Amun, the previously revered deity. As she grew up, Ankhesenamun didn't simply stand by while this upheaval played out; instead, she learned the ropes of navigating political storms. It must have been like learning how to dance in a hurricane without spilling your drink. By the time her father had transformed Egypt's worship practices, Ankhesenamun had developed a keen sense of political adaptability, which ensured that she could maintain her footing no matter how rough things got.

When her half-brother, Tutankhamun, rose to power at the tender age of nine, Ankhesenamun—around 13 at the time—married him, acting as both his wife and his partner in statecraft (DeLong, 2023). Now, here were two young royals, barely teenagers, who were expected to run a country. Anchored in this reality, their marriage was a political alliance designed to restore stability to a kingdom in theological turmoil. The duo worked together to pivot Egypt back toward traditional beliefs, with Ankhesenamun playing a vital role in steering these religious renovations.

Check Mate

Palace walls never shielded anyone completely from external politics. Ankhesenamun, another chess master in the diplomatic game, proved shrewd in interacting with powerful figures beyond Egypt's borders. With Tutankhamun's sudden death, she faced a difficult situation thanks to having no heir to the throne and her land being vulnerable to instability. Legend has it that she reached out to Šuppiluliuma I, king of the Hittites, an ancient kingdom in modern-day Turkey, requesting one of his sons as a new husband to secure her position and Egypt's future (Jarus, 2023). It was radical, unexpected, and decidedly clever. By today's standards, it would be like sending an email to your fiercest competitor asking for job security!

The path wasn't smooth from then on, yet Ankhesenamun didn't falter in her pursuit of stability. She married Ay, a senior advisor who succeeded Tutankhamun as pharaoh. This marriage wasn't borne out of love but out of necessity. It was a strategic alliance meant to legitimize Ay's claim to the throne and ensure Ankhesenamun's survival in a court rife with intrigue. The choices she made might seem desperate, but they underline her resilience and determination to remain influential despite shifting sands.

Ankhesenamun's Legacy

But why should we care about these events today? Because Ankhesenamun's story isn't just history; it's a tale of enduring tenacity. For you and other young women around the world grappling with challenges, her legacy is a beacon of courage. In a time when gender roles were rigidly defined, she defied them, demonstrating that strength and intelligence aren't bound by tradition.

Her tale might have faded into obscurity if not for moments of audacious bravery. At every turn, Ankhesenamun did what needed to be done, embracing change and confronting crises head-on. Her legacy might well remind us that even when we are faced with overwhelming odds, the choices we make with both head and heart leave unforgettable marks.

Mediating with powerful figures is an art Ankhesenamun was adept at. Think of it as negotiating for backstage passes at the biggest concert of your life, only the stakes are the fate of an entire nation. What she did required sharp wit, diplomacy, and the ability to read the room better than most. For you as an aspiring leader, the takeaway is clear: Sometimes, securing support is less about wielding power and more about enlisting allies.

Let's embrace the inspiration we've drawn from Ankhesenamun's presence during a transformative period in Egyptian history. Her saga is a lesson in how leveraging our position in times of peril often involves creativity, collaboration, and the courage to reach across divisions. Although we might not face the same trials today, the principles of adaptability, alliance-building, and bravery still resonate deeply. Her actions whisper wisdom across centuries, inviting us to redefine limits and explore possibilities beyond the thrones of our own lives.

Conclusion

After our whirlwind tour of ancient Egyptian queens, it's clear that these royal women knew how to play the game and win big, all while draped in fabulous regalia. From Tiye's diplomatic high-wire acts to Nefertari's architectural feats and Ankhesenamun's deft political moves, each queen set herself apart on the stone walls and papyrus scrolls of history that continue to whisper their tales. They weren't just figures standing behind their pharaohs; they were trailblazers who bent the rules and redefined what it meant to be powerful. These stories show that being a woman in a man's world can be less about fitting in and more about flipping the script.

For you young dreamers and leaders, these women serve as shimmering mirrors reflecting courage, intellect, and the occasional sneaky strategy. There's plenty of royal wisdom to glean from our three queens, like knowing when to call the shots directly or when to rally your squad for support. So, here's to you and all the other girls and women navigating life's challenges: May you wield your influence creatively, build alliances boldly, and never underestimate the power of a well-placed metaphorical chess move. Who knows? You might just find your name etched in monuments—or at least in the hearts of those inspired by you.

Chapter 5:

Warriors and Leaders—Leading With Courage

Reflecting on the history of courage takes us on a colorful journey back to ancient Egypt, where the sandals of leadership, traditionally adorning kings, were occasionally worn by queens like Ahhotep I and Neithhotep. These women navigated the political and military landscapes of their times the way you might maneuver a chariot through a bustling bazaar.

In this chapter, you'll discover how Ahhotep deftly managed both battles and alliances during her reign. Far from just ruling from the sidelines, she grabbed history by the horns—or, rather, by the hilt of a sword—and left quite a mark on her kingdom. Meanwhile, Neithhotep's name echoes through time as a symbol of female influence in military affairs, providing historians today with a delightful labyrinth of clues to unravel. But wait, there's more! This chapter doesn't just rest on the laurels of battle-hardened queens; it also dives into the fascinating myth of Nitocris, a ruler whose reality blurs with legend, and explores her alleged feats and dramatic tales of flood-induced justice.

By weaving together threads of historical fact, speculation, and a dash of myth, this chapter showcases how these women broke barriers and redefined what it meant to lead in ancient Egypt. It shines a spotlight on their martial prowess and statesmanship, offering you a rich narrative filled with empowering examples of female leadership. You'll voyage through tales of decisive battles, clever strategies, and the kind of governance that could make even the Sphinx crack a smile. So, buckle up for a fun-filled exploration of ancient female warriors and leaders who rewrote the rules of their world and left plenty of inspiration to draw upon.

Ahhotep I

The tale of Ahhotep I unfolds during the tumultuous, sometimes chaotic, Ahmose Dynasty. Ahhotep was born into a world where every royal decision could determine the fate of the kingdom. But her story goes beyond mere survival under the threat of foreign invasion; it is about strategic brilliance and the unexpected rise of female leadership in a predominantly male sphere.

Let's put ourselves in Ahhotep's shoes for a moment, imagining the vivid sounds of bustling Thebes and what it must have been like navigating the political labyrinth of alliances and enemy threats. With the untimely death of her husband, Seqenenre Tao, who'd fallen in battle against the Hyksos, the mantle of leadership found its way to Ahhotep. Now, how does a woman in this position face such a challenge? Well, Ahhotep stepped up with gusto, filling the void left by her husband and guiding her kingdom through perilous times. In the face of Hyksos aggression from the north and Nubian threats from the south, her leadership qualities shone brightly.

Leading From the Front

Ahhotep's proactive choices, defying the expectations placed upon women at the time, send a strong message that greatness can arise from anywhere. Through her decisive actions, she challenged the gender stereotypes prevalent in governance. Far from being a passive regent, she demonstrated that commanding a nation wasn't just a man's prerogative. This determination showed that she was more than capable of steering Egypt through rough waters.

Her accomplishments didn't stop at merely safeguarding the throne. Ahhotep played a pivotal role in rallying the military during the expulsion of the Hyksos, a contribution that redefined the perception of women in military history. She led from the front, proving that you don't need to be a warrior to possess the spirit of one. Under her guidance, the Egyptian forces were consolidated and invigorated, marking the beginning of a new chapter in their struggle against foreign dominance. Her efforts helped initiate successes that led to the eventual reunification of Egypt under her son, Ahmose I.

A Lesson in Resilience

By refusing to crumble under pressure, Ahhotep set an example that transcends her era, providing a timeless testament to perseverance. Her leadership reminds us that setbacks are often just setups for comebacks. Through her unwavering resolve, she carved out a space in history for all women who would follow in her footsteps, proving that strength doesn't always wear armor.

Ahhotep I's Legacy

Recognition came to Ahhotep both in life and in death. Her valor was honored with military accolades, notably found among her grave goods, which were quite unusual for women of her time. A stela—a stone slab—in the temple at Karnak immortalizes her feats, acknowledging her wisdom in governance and her crucial role in calming warring factions. These tokens marked a definitive shift in how contributions to warfare and governance could be recognized, regardless of gender.

Even after her death, Ahhotep's impact resonated throughout Egypt. Her memory has inspired generations, and because it speaks volumes about the potential of women in positions of power, her story still holds significant weight. Her influence reached far beyond the battles of ancient Egypt, showing future leaders that authenticity, courage, and determination are key factors for impactful leadership.

For young women today, Ahhotep stands as a figure of empowerment. Her life is a resounding call to action for you and others aspiring to make a societal impact, and her example encourages you to embrace challenges head-on, just like Ahhotep did when facing an uncertain future. Her journey is a reflection of how true leadership often emerges in the most unexpected ways and from the most unexpected characters.

As we reflect on Ahhotep's legacy, remember that her story isn't just about ancient warfare or dynastic politics. It's about breaking barriers, redefining roles, and paving the way for new understandings of what courage could look like. Through her example, you might find the inspiration to step into roles you might not have envisioned for yourself and drive change in the world you inhabit.

Neithhotep

As our next queen shows, the significance of noble heritage cannot be overstressed, as it provided opportunities for women to hold power and participate actively in governance. Born into a prominent family, Neithhotep's lineage set the stage for her influential position in society. Her association with royalty, likely through her marriage to King Narmer, further solidified her status and influence during the First Dynasty, when the foundations of the Egyptian state were being laid.

A stroll through history brings to light fascinating archaeological artifacts linked to Neithhotep, hinting at her possible participation in military defense. These relics, including seals and inscriptions bearing her name, suggest that she may have played a role in protecting her realm during turbulent times. It's tempting to imagine her donning armor, leading troops, or strategizing battle plans, but all we have are glimpses through these silent witnesses from the past. Regardless, these symbols of authority reflect her potential involvement in ensuring the safety and stability of her kingdom, challenging any assumptions that women were simply passive observers in ancient warfare.

Underappreciated by History

A critique of how women's roles have been understated is vital to appreciating their true legacy, and the evidence surrounding Neithhotep's life and legacy is a great example of why this is so essential. Ancient texts, although often cryptic, provide valuable insights into how she was portrayed by her contemporaries. Understanding these accounts requires a critical eye, especially since historical narratives tend to underplay or overlook the contributions of women. According to some interpretations, Neithhotep's presence in royal annals and monuments emphasizes her importance, yet her story remains somewhat shrouded in mystery (Ancient World Hub, 2024).

As we sift through the layers of time, the depiction of Neithhotep in ancient texts emerges as a focal point for examining gender biases in historical narratives. These accounts, laden with symbolism and nuance, reflect not only her stature but also the limitations male-dominated storytelling traditions have imposed on her. The task of unearthing her true influence involves questioning these portrayals, seeking to read between the lines of what was recorded and what was left unsaid. By doing so, we can reclaim Neithhotep's rightful place among Egypt's architects of power and change.

Neithhotep's Legacy

The resonance of Neithhotep's name and title as queen over time speaks to the enduring impact of her legacy. Her name, possibly linking her to the war goddess Neith, evokes images of feminine strength and wisdom. This symbolic connection affirms her authority and reflects her high rank, serving as a testament to the recognition of her leadership capabilities. That we are talking about her now is proof that Neithhotep's legacy transcends her lifetime and continues to influence how subsequent generations perceive and embrace the idea of women in positions of power.

Neithhotep's story embodies both the challenges and triumphs of female leadership in ancient Egypt, offering you and other young women an empowering reflection of your potential. Analyzing her role as a high-ranking warrior uncovers a story that resonates with themes of empowerment, resilience, and equality—values that are ever-relevant today.

Understanding the broader context of Neithhotep's era enhances the appreciation of her contributions. During this formative phase of Egyptian civilization, the emergence of centralized power structures demanded skillful governance. This environment allowed powerful women like Neithhotep, who were guided by their intellectual prowess and strategic thinking, to rise within political and social hierarchies. Her inclusion in the pages of history as a potential coregent or advisor reflects the progressive nature of leadership dynamics in early Egypt, challenging the patriarchal norms prevalent in many other ancient cultures of that era and those of later Egyptian dynasties.

Artifacts attributed to Neithhotep, such as ceremonial items, reinforce the notion that she held considerable sway in religious and civic affairs. These objects bear witness to her capacity to impact spiritual and cultural life, positioning her as a figure of deep reverence. Each artifact tells a story—a silent testimony to her role in shaping the social practices and political landscape of her time. They invite us to speculate on the ceremonies she might have overseen, the oaths that would have been sworn under her guidance, and the decisions that influenced Egypt's early identity.

The enduring legacy of this queen provides a metaphorical compass guiding us toward a more nuanced understanding of leadership. That we still remember her name is a reminder that the essence of true leadership lies in courage, vision, and the willingness to transcend boundaries. Her story is an affirmation that historical narratives can and should include the diverse voices of those whose stories illuminate pathways of strength and determination.

Nitocris

Nitocris, a name veiled in mystery, has sparked curiosity for centuries. She is often depicted as one of the earliest female rulers of ancient

Egypt despite the blurred lines between legend and reality. Her story is so captivating that it paints an enthralling picture of power and resilience, one interwoven with the dynamic landscape of ancient Egyptian lore.

Separating Fact From Fiction

The legendary ascent of Nitocris demonstrates how history and mythology often merge, creating narratives that withstand the test of time. According to the Greek historian Manetho, Nitocris took the throne after avenging her brother's murder by flooding a banquet hall with the Nile and drowning those who were responsible for his death (Mark, 2017d). This depiction of her dramatic rise to power, though likely fictional, captures the imagination and is an example of the fascinating way in which tales from the past are shaped. Her supposed actions, though perhaps more storytelling than truth, showcase elements of governance intertwined with justice.

Examining the tales of Nitocris's rule allows us to explore the leadership strategies attributed to her. While historical evidence about her reign remains scarce, stories about her offer insights into the decision-making processes of the time. Ancient narratives often present her as a ruler who didn't shy away from making bold choices. That these tales have been passed on from one generation to the next reflects an appreciation for decisiveness and cunning in leadership—timeless qualities that transcend gender and era. Such legends suggest that even in ancient times, where documentation was limited, the valorization of strong leadership traits in women existed, at least in the mythological realm.

Nitocris's Legacy

Nitocris's cultural impact extends far beyond her mythical deeds. Her tale serves as a precursor to portrayals of other formidable female rulers in Egypt, like Cleopatra and Hatshepsut. Each of these figures carved out a distinct legacy within a male-dominated world. By casting Nitocris in roles that highlight strength and decisiveness, the narratives about her challenge and expand on traditional depictions of women leaders. The continued fascination with stories about powerful women also underscores their role in shaping how cultures understand and relate to concepts of female authority.

Comparing the trials Nitocris faced and the struggles women today confront provides a modern context for her story. Her legend resonates with the ongoing journey toward gender equality, and it can also serve as inspiration for aspiring leaders. Nitocris embodies not only the challenges you may have to overcome in asserting your place but also the potential to triumph over adversity. The blend of myth and metaphor speaks volumes about the universal struggle for recognition and autonomy we as women have experienced throughout history.

You can use mythical tales like the ones about Nitocris as tools for empowerment and education. They encourage critical thinking about historical narratives while inspiring you to embrace qualities like courage and innovation. As you dissect and analyze myths, understanding their intrinsic value becomes vital to appreciating how they serve as a catalyst for dialogue on current issues.

Conclusion

As we conclude another leg of our journey through the painted halls of ancient Egypt's finest temples, let's take a moment to salute some fierce female warriors and leaders. Ahhotep I took charge like a boss, managing to fend off threats from all sides while making sure her royal duties didn't crumble like an old ruin. She proved that you didn't need to wear a pointy headdress to rule (but hey, it probably looked cool). With every bold decision she made, Ahhotep knocked down gender barriers faster than a tumbleweed rolling across the Nile. Her legacy is like a well-preserved hieroglyphic—clear and powerful, showing future queens that flexible thinking beats fancy armor any day.

Speaking of queens, Neithhotep didn't come to play either. In the land of pyramids and papyrus scrolls, she carved out her own legendary path. While we can only guess whether she was rocking Egyptian eyeliner in battle or planning logistical coups, one thing's for sure: Her influence lingers on like the smell of freshly baked date bread. And let's not forget the mythical mystery that was Nitocris. Today, young women everywhere can look at these tales and think, *If they could do it, so can I!* Whether you're stepping into leadership roles or just trying to charge your way through algebra class, remember—these ladies did it in sandals, so surely, we can do it in sneakers!

Chapter 6:

Unraveling Scientific Mysteries

Get ready to step into an era where the sun casts its golden rays onto queens and ordinary women whose stories have been buried under layers of both time and misconception. Transporting you through the ages to uncover long-hidden secrets and discover truths that have been all but forgotten, this chapter shines the spotlight on ancient Egyptian women who have been mesmerizing enigmas for centuries. It answers the question: What about the women who stood beside powerful Egyptian men, weaving their own legacies in the shadows of towering pyramids?

In this next stage of our adventure, modern scientific advancements take center stage, shedding light on these women's lives, roles, and health. We look into genetic studies that unravel the threads of royal lineages and reshape historical narratives with every discovery. You'll find yourself immersed in tales of Egyptian queens who commanded respect and wielded power, challenging long-standing stereotypes with each revelation. With the aid of new-age technologies like CT scans, we explore the truths behind their everyday experiences, from health issues that resonate with us today to the complex societal webs they navigated. It's time for a captivating journey that redefines what we know about these ancient dynastic influencers, one that invites us to see how their stories mirror and inspire our own quests for empowerment in the present day.

How DNA Studies Help Us Understand Royal Lineages

Modern DNA research is like a time machine for uncovering whispers from the past, and it has landed us smack in the middle of ancient Egypt. The hush-hush world of royal politics, family squabbles, and lady bosses that ruled the Nile has started to unravel thread by thread, thanks to genetic detectives wielding Y-DNA and mitochondrial DNA analysis.

Picture the blinding sun rising over towering monuments, casting shadows as long-lasting as the Egyptian dynasties themselves. At this point, you know that although pharaohs stamped their names in stone and strolled around with equally impressive headwear, it was the women in their lives who often held the key to power. Now, modern science is pulling back the curtain on their impact, showing us how maternal lines traced through Y-DNA and mitochondrial DNA are redefining lineage and legacy.

The Ties That Bind

In ancient Egypt, family ties were like a game of divine Jenga. As we dive into the genetic pool of figures like Hatshepsut and Nefertiti, we see how they reshaped dynasties, challenging traditional roles that once seemed set in stone. Hatshepsut's ruling prowess, for instance, was more than a mere footnote in history. Her matrilineal connections reveal a map that turns the tables on tradition. Her deliberate positioning of her daughter, Neferura, mirrored her own ascent, highlighting the importance of female lineages in maintaining dynastic stability (Belmonte, 2022).

Enter Nefertiti, another queen whose DNA story sheds light on her powerful role. Her influence isn't just measured by her iconic bust but by her potential familial ties to influential rulers. Based on recent interpretations of DNA data, her connection to Akhenaten, her husband, challenges past narratives. It raises questions about the interconnectedness of their joint reign and the potential for shared governance (Robinson, 2020).

The Missing Link

DNA findings also bridge the gap between old-world health perceptions and modern genetic insights. Imagine stumbling upon an ancient artifact only to find it holds clues to today's medical conditions! This genetic bridge lets us peek into the health issues historical women faced, linking them to present concerns. Well-preserved remains provide genetic material that offers glimpses into everything from hereditary diseases to dietary habits. Modern technology has unveiled conditions like osteoporosis or arthritis that plagued ancient, mummified leaders, reminding us that some struggles are timeless.

Beyond the insights they provide on personal health, these discoveries also shatter long-standing assumptions about women's roles in ancient history. For centuries, historians viewed the narrative of men leading and women supporting as unshakable. But tracing maternal DNA reveals complexities suggesting that Egyptian queens wielded significant power and influence. Their stories reflect bold decisions and strategic moves that impacted not only their immediate lineage but also the course of history itself.

One compelling aspect is how these revelations challenge our perception of leadership. In today's context, where conversations revolve around empowering women and breaking glass ceilings, these ancient figures serve as beacons of strength and influence. They encourage us to think deeply about how such roles have evolved over millennia, nudging young women like you to find inspiration in the past while charting your path for the future.

This newfound understanding invites us to rethink entrenched narratives and embrace a broader view of history that celebrates complexity. By shining a light on the matrilineal influence, DNA research reminds us of the power within seemingly quiet forces. These women navigated choppy waters, commanded respect, and left a lasting impact—whether or not historians were initially willing to acknowledge it.

As we connect the dots between ancient genetic puzzles and current scientific advancements, it's clear that women's contributions transcend eras. This intersection of gender studies and historical inquiry opens doors to conversations about equality, leadership, and societal impact. Future generations can draw lessons from these pioneers who fought battles both visible and behind the scenes, leaving legacies that resonate even now.

How Mummy Research Has Affected Knowledge of Women's Health

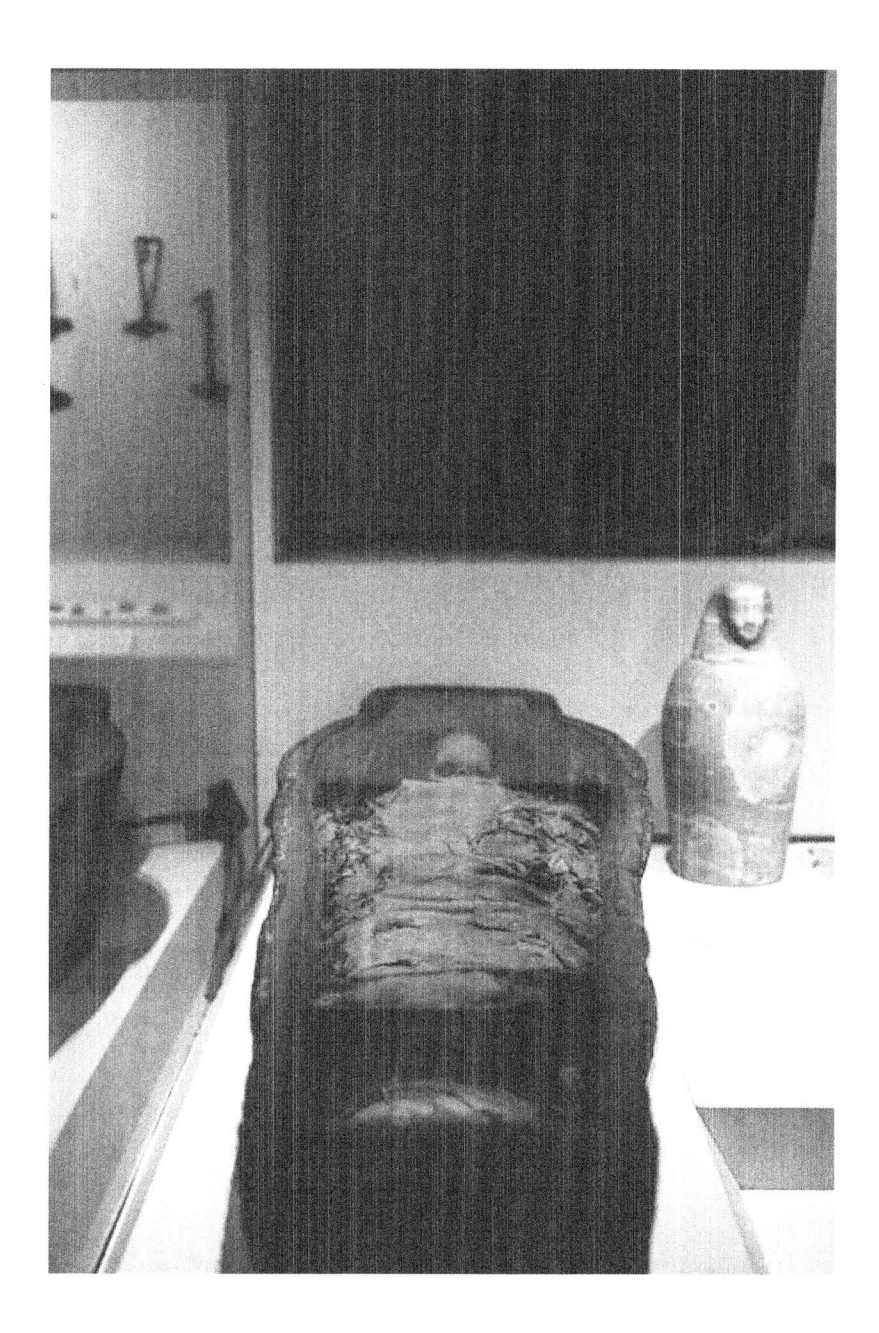

Thanks to science, the story of ancient Egyptian women is coming to life and revealing secrets we've never been privy to. It allows us to venture down the bustling streets of ancient Egypt, where women strolled past grand temples and through vibrant marketplaces, their lives hidden from us for centuries. Now, thanks to advancements like CT scans and imaging techniques, we're unearthing the mysteries of these enigmatic figures.

A Glimpse Into the Unknown

CT scans and other noninvasive technologies are game changers, allowing us to peer inside mummies without disturbing their eternal rest. These tools have unveiled the hidden ailments that plagued women, casting them as active agents navigating the medical landscape of their time. For instance, evidence of dental issues like tooth loss and severe attrition shows that, even back then, the need for trips to the dentist was far from rare. These discoveries highlight that the need for health care, much like our own visits to the orthodontist or dentist today, has always been prevalent (GE Healthcare, 2005).

But it's not just about teeth! Consider the skeletal X-rays revealing osteophytes in the spine—a fancy way of saying bone spurs—that paint a picture of common ailments potentially caused by hard labor or age-related conditions. These details bring to light the struggles and resilience of royal women, disputing stereotypes that might portray them as passive queens lounging on chaise lounges. They were real people with real concerns, reminding us that some things, like back pain, never change.

Ancient Nutrition

Now let's chat about food—who doesn't love that topic? As young historians in the making, consider how often diet reflects cultural exchange and economic status, even in your daily choices. From quinoa salads casually dominating lunch menus to avocados topping toast, our plates also tell complex stories of class and connectivity.

Nutritional analyses of mummified remains serve up surprising revelations about diet and status. You'd think rich diets were reserved only for those dripping in gold, right? Wrong! Analyzing hair and bones has indicated varied diets that challenge the social assumptions of who got the best meals at the dining table. As it turns out, nutrition was intimately linked to personal health management (SaadEl-Din, 2023). This fresh perspective allows us to regard ancient dietary habits not as static norms but as dynamic practices influenced by various factors, such as trade, which introduced new foods.

Embalming Practices

Speaking of complexity, let's venture into the fascinating world of embalming practices. How women were mummified tells a tale of how their societal roles extended beyond life itself. Studying these sacred rites reveals both reverence and bias. A notable example is the absence of organ removal in certain female burials, a deviation from typical male mummification processes (GE Healthcare, 2005). Was this because they weren't as "worthy" of full-on post-mortem TLC? Or perhaps it highlighted unique cultural beliefs about women's purity.

When we investigate further, we learn that the luxurious ingredients used during embalming, like exotic frankincense and juniper oil, offer insights into a woman's social standing. The more opulent the materials, the higher the likelihood the woman enjoyed an elevated status in her community, like having a VIP pass to the party of the past. It's intriguing how things like wigs, sometimes made with imported human hair, played into this narrative, adding layers (pun intended) to understanding what these objects signified about beauty standards and identity.

Finally, let's not forget the renowned female mummies. These well-preserved figures aren't just relics; they're portals into unique pasts that ignite our curiosity. For example, who was the Screaming Woman? When she was discovered mid-shriek, was she voicing her displeasure and preserved that way for eternity, or was she simply caught at an awkward camera angle of her time? Stories like hers are intriguing, bringing these women closer to us not as distant historical characters

69

but as relatable human beings with complexities and contributions worth exploring.

How Science Challenges Previous Narratives

In the rich history of ancient Egypt, women played roles as varied and intricate as a scarab beetle's wing pattern. Yet, much like those wings, their stories have often been hidden beneath layers of dust and misconception. Modern scientific advancements are peeling back these layers to reveal a clearer, more inclusive picture of what life was like for these women, overriding old myths and assumptions in the process.

For centuries, the images conjured of Egyptian queens were largely shaped by hieroglyphics on temple walls or worn-out papyrus scrolls. These pieces of evidence were interpreted through a narrow lens that saw them primarily as wives or mothers living in the shadow of mighty pharaohs. Recent findings, fueled by cutting-edge technologies and interdisciplinary research, are flipping this script, though. Through archaeological digs, genetic analysis, and anthropological insights, we now understand that women in ancient Egypt occupied spaces far beyond their domestic confines: They were priests, landowners, and even rulers.

Redefining Gender Roles

One particularly fascinating insight from modern science is how DNA evidence and skeletal studies debunk long-standing stereotypes about gender roles. For instance, genetic testing has confirmed that tombs once presumed to belong to men due to the grave goods found within them, like weapons, actually belong to women. Beyond challenging our assumptions, this also encourages critical thought about accepted narratives around marginalized figures. It's a cheeky reminder not to judge a burial by its baubles alone!

The narrative shift doesn't stop with the bones. It extends into the realm of how these discoveries come to light. Consider the remarkable contributions of women scientists leading the charge in these revelations. If you yearn for role models who reflect empowerment and equality, their work will no doubt resonate powerfully with you. Good examples of this are Dr. Zahi Hawass, an archaeologist known for her fervent excavation zeal, alongside emerging female Egyptologists who display their own aspirations for leadership and societal impact.

Using Multiple Approaches

By leveraging interdisciplinary approaches, researchers seamlessly weave together archaeology, genetics, and anthropology to create a richer, more textured understanding of history's landscape. In one study, geneticists teamed up with archaeologists to map out familial relations across tomb complexes, unveiling connections that weren't clear from textual sources or artifacts alone (The Archaeologist, 2023). These collaborations are akin to historic jam sessions where different instruments come together to create a harmonious symphony of discovery.

But why does this matter today? Well, it's not just about rewriting history books; it's about shaping conversations in our current era, too. These new findings intersect with ongoing discussions around gender equality, pushing us to rethink the dynamics of social justice movements. Ancient dialogues of women's power and influence resonate with modern efforts toward gender equity, showing how timeless these themes are.

Influence on Modern Perceptions

It's easy to see how shifting our perception of ancient Egyptian women can influence contemporary understandings. By recognizing the dynamic roles these women occupied, we challenge today's biases and pave the way for a broader acceptance of diverse identities. In other words, learning that Amenhotep's sister might have led a religious cult not only excites our inner history buff but also adds momentum to the push for gender-inclusive discussions in classrooms. This is a glorious opportunity to remind ourselves that history is not fixed; it's a living conversation that is continually informed by new voices and perspectives.

In this intriguing mix of archaeological passion and feminist insight, it's important to include guidelines on integrating these narratives into contemporary discussions. Approach these new findings with a critical mind and encourage questions that pursue the deeper meanings behind them rather than simply accepting surface-level interpretations. This approach ensures that each discovery feeds into a broader understanding of gender roles, past and present.

So, let us relish the irony that while ancient Egyptians perfected eye makeup and pyramid construction, it took millennia—and lots of DNA testing—to finally give their women the recognition they deserved. These scientific breakthroughs redefine what we know, challenging entrenched myths and opening doors to inspiring discussions about who writes history and, more importantly, who gets to read it.

Conclusion

As we emerge from the dusty corridors of the long-ago past into the bright lights of scientific exploration, it's worth appreciating how our adventure through ancient Egypt has continued to reveal how important women were in shaping this iconic historical period. We've pulled back the tomb lids, dusted off some bones, and found that Egyptian women weren't just baking bread or dressing for the latest pyramid gala—they were leaders, influencers, and trendsetters. With DNA research and futuristic gadgets like CT scans, these women are no longer whispers on papyruses but powerful voices shouting across the ages. Their stories challenge the old narratives, showing us that they were as complex and vibrant as the fabrics used to wrap them in eternal slumber.

With this refreshed lens, we're no longer just peeking into the past; we're forging connections between the past and present that can inspire you as an aspiring leader. Whether it's Hatshepsut's bold moves or Nefertiti's strategic brilliance, the figures we've encountered throughout each chapter offer lessons in resilience and courage, which are essential for any ambitious mind navigating through their own personal deserts. So, let's keep digging and questioning. Who knows how many more secrets these ancient tales hold? Just remember—history is a work in progress, much like our journey toward acknowledging every voice that has ever graced it.

Chapter 7:

Spiritual Lives—Women in Religion and Belief

An investigation into the spiritual lives of women in ancient Egypt is filled with unexpected plot twists and fascinating characters. The priestesses strolling through temple corridors, although adorned in intricate jewelry, were also carrying the weight of cosmic order on their shoulders. These women played roles that transcended mere ceremony—they were conduits, connecting the earthly to the divine and commanding rituals that were said to keep the universe humming.

With every chant and offering, they ensured the essential balance of life was maintained. Their indispensable contribution seemed, quite frankly, a little stressful. Imagine messing up a sacred ritual and being blamed for universal chaos! Yet priestesses did more than maintain harmony; they wielded real influence, guiding communities with grace and authority that made them unforgettable.

As you approach this chapter, get ready to uncover stories of how female spiritual leaders balanced power and femininity in a world dominated by men. You'll discover how noblewomen ascended to significant roles in religious structures, signaling both privilege and responsibility, and you'll journey inside the secretive, candle-lit chambers where female oracles shared words that could alter the course of political destinies.

However, while the chants and ceremonies were important, our real interest is in understanding how these women shaped society and influenced history. With that in mind, you'll also learn about how social status and spiritual leadership intersected and witness the dynamic way priestesses managed temples like they were holy headquarters. Now, brace yourself, because you're about to step into the intriguing world of ancient Egyptian belief systems, where women were vital players who left legacies that echo into modern discussions on gender and empowerment.

Priestesses: The Temple Activities

Priestesses weren't just hanging around temples looking pretty with their fancy headdresses and elaborate accessories. No, they were the rock stars of religious life, orchestrating the daily rituals that kept the balance of the universe in check. Just consider the stress of holding a job where your main task is to keep the cosmic order from tipping into chaos—that'll have you appreciating the roles these women played real quick. Priestesses also actively participated in purification ceremonies and offerings, ensuring that Ma'at, the divine harmony essential to Egyptian belief, was observed at all times. This responsibility was not just for show; it was believed to be critical for the world's stability. Supposedly, if you skipped a sacred chant or two, you'd mess up the whole balance of things. No pressure!

Conduits for the Gods

Priestesses, serving as intermediaries between the gods and the people, wielded considerable influence within their communities. With chants and prayers echoing through stone halls, they conducted rituals that helped maintain spiritual connections with the divine. If you were an ancient Egyptian, you'd likely see these priestesses playing a vital role during temple festivals, too. Their presence was central to community celebrations, where they didn't just blend into the background. They led processions, performed sacred dances, and sang hymns believed to invite blessings and protection from the deities. Through these special occasions, priestesses reinforced their societal importance and visibility. Everyone knew their names, not just because they threw fabulous events but because they were seen as vital connectors to higher powers.

The Chosen Ones

Becoming a priestess wasn't like accidentally stumbling across a golden ticket. It was almost like being handpicked to be part of a secret club, only this one involved less cloak-wearing and more chanting in front of altars. Noblewomen were often favored, lending an air of exclusivity to the role, so being born into the right family certainly had its perks. The inclusion of women of a higher rank also highlights the intersection of social status and religious authority in ancient Egypt, suggesting that spiritual leadership was a privilege that was closely linked to lineage. But there was more to it than just bloodline. It also spoke volumes about how women were perceived in terms of capability and trust in managing religious duties.

When it came to their day-to-day duties, priestesses weren't just doing some light housekeeping; they were basically running full-on operations. They ensured that the temple operated smoothly, doing everything from organizing staff to overseeing the maintenance of complex rituals. Temples weren't your average places of worship either—they were considered the literal homes of the gods. It would have been like trying to keep a celestial Airbnb tidy for some rather picky guests. That's what priestesses did, day in and day out. In doing so, they held significant power, as only those involved with the divine had access to knowledge and influences beyond the everyday experiences of common people.

An Exclusive Club

The appointment of women hailing from noble families also addressed a broader respect for women's capabilities in religious and societal structures. It acknowledged women as vital players in maintaining the link between the gods and humanity, which is evidence of empowerment within an otherwise male-dominated ancient society. Priestesses played their roles with a weight of authority and skill that affirmed their competence and importance in sustaining religious practices.

As spiritual leaders, they empowered other women within the community by setting examples of leadership and dedication. Whether performing a ritual or leading a festival, priestesses stood at the forefront of public life, providing young girls and women with tangible role models who blended intelligence, spirituality, and power. It was less about wielding a scepter and more about demonstrating strength and influence—a concept that we can definitely appreciate as modern women.

The Influence of Female Oracles

Female oracles played an extraordinary role in ancient Egypt, bringing an air of wisdom and mystery into tales of days past. These seers who whispered secrets of the future were significant political figures, operating as advisors who could tip the scales of power with a few prophetic words. Leaders, often kings, turned to them when faced with important decisions. In a time when divine endorsement was essential for governance, their insights were perceived as coming directly from the gods, making them indispensable in the societal hierarchy.

Guidance From the Gods

The oracles' predictions impacted political strategy and shaped societal norms. For instance, a prophecy might encourage a pharaoh to embark on military campaigns or initiate diplomatic marriages. Decisions like these were guided by the oracle's ability to interpret the divine messages she received through complex rituals, ceremonies, or dreams. Picture yourself standing in the grand halls where these seers declared their visions while leaders anxiously awaited a nod from the gods. This reverence afforded these women a uniquely powerful position that transcended the typical gender roles of their era.

However, oracles were both respected and feared. Their profound connection with the divine placed them in a category of their own, separate from ordinary women and even distinct from other religious officials. This classification highlights the fluidity and complexity of their gender roles. They embodied a duality—they were women navigating a male-dominated society while also commanding respect and fear due to their sacred duties. This twofold nature made them figures of both empowerment and mystique, often straddling the line between mortal advisors and godlike beings.

A Cut Above the Rest

Central to the role of an oracle were her ceremonial duties, which underscored her authority within religious practices. These duties were vital rituals that bound the spiritual and earthly realms. The elaborate ceremonies that might involve trance-like states or communication with deities were believed to be instrumental in maintaining the cosmic balance. Such responsibilities signified the oracles' indispensable presence in the religious landscape, elevating them to positions of power not typically accessible to women at the time.

A glimpse into history reveals tales of formidable female oracles who left unforgettable marks on society. The Temple of Amun in Karnak is a notable example of a sacred place where these women exerted tremendous influence. Here, their declarations were pivotal in shaping state policies and royal decisions. Perhaps among the most captivating stories is that of Pharaoh Hatshepsut, who legitimized her rule by claiming divine selection by the god Amun through an oracle's message. By doing so, she redefined norms and solidified her status using the proclamation as divine approval (Kubisch, 2023).

The Isis Cult

The incredible journey of Isis, the Egyptian goddess known for her magic and nurturing abilities that we encountered in Chapter 2, transcended borders as she became a universal deity worshipped far beyond the banks of the Nile. Her association with motherhood, protection, and magic made her an appealing figure to various cultures across time and space. As stories of her prowess and compassionate nature traveled, so did the influence of female divinity, pushing cultural boundaries and fostering new spiritual blends.

Isis's role extended beyond the protective mother, as she was also seen as a wise healer and a powerful force in times of need. This made her relatable and beloved, enabling her worship to easily transcend geographic constraints. Long before social media could make someone worldwide famous, Isis's reputation spread through trade routes and conquests, reaching distant lands and integrating into new societies.

Isis Goes Viral

Temples dedicated to Isis began to appear internationally, from Greece to Rome and even as far as England, serving as beacons of her presence and underscoring her broad appeal. These sites, often situated in bustling cities and trade hubs of the ancient world, became centers of worship where people from different walks of life could gather to honor the goddess. Their existence highlighted her growing influence as a symbol of female divinity. They stood as testaments to her universal appeal, further asserting her role as a protector and nurturer.

Cultural adaptations took root as Isis worship mingled with local traditions, creating unique blends that were both region-specific and continuous over time. In Greece, for example, she was associated with Demeter and Persephone, while in Rome, she enjoyed connections with Hecate and Diana, illustrating how her qualities resonated across cultures. As these intersections occurred, they created a diverse mix of spiritual practices that included elements of native customs and beliefs interwoven with Isis's divine narrative. This adaptability allowed her cult to thrive amid shifting political landscapes and changing local customs, sustaining her legacy through the ages.

The lasting impact of the Cult of Isis is still evident today, continuing to inspire modern interpretations of female empowerment and spirituality. Current feminist movements sometimes draw parallels between the strength and resilience of Isis and modern ideas of womanhood and leadership. By looking back at her enduring legacy, you can find solace and inspiration, seeing her as a reflection of your own aspirations for equality, power, and respect.

Conclusion

Throughout this chapter, we've uncovered the fascinating world of women in spiritual orders in ancient Egypt. These ladies were much more than just footnotes in history. They were the A-listers of their temples and societies! As priestesses, they juggled cosmic responsibilities like daily prayers, channeling divine energy through dance and making sure everything ran as smoothly as a Nile barge. They orchestrated elaborate rituals and led grand festivals. Their influence was immense, with noblewomen often filling these roles, showcasing both lineage prestige and women's real knack for maintaining sacred duties. With power stitched into their headdresses, they stood tall as symbols of wisdom and commitment, showing their communities that women could lead, thank you very much.

We also met the all-knowing oracles, whose mystical insights steered politics and made pharaohs sit up and listen. Imagine holding such authority that even kings would heed your whispers from the gods! These influential women navigated through the male-centric society, all while holding on to their unique blend of mystery and might. And as if priestesses and oracles weren't already busy enough rewriting the rules, the Cult of Isis came bursting onto the scene. This goddess went viral long before the age of Instagram influencers, leaving her mark across lands with tales of nurturing motherhood and unmatched magic. Together, these women wove a narrative of empowerment and stand as timeless icons you can turn to for inspiration today.

Chapter 8:

Love, Passion, and Power Dynamics

Love, passion, and power dynamics have swaggered their way through the sands of ancient Egypt, leaving behind tales that would give even the most dramatic soap operas a run for their money. Romance in this era was not just about batting eyelashes or exchanging love-laden papyrus notes. It was an elaborate kaleidoscope of myths, societal structures, and the occasional cosmic intrigue. To the ancient Egyptians, love was the stuff of legendary stories that shaped their society and echoed through mudbrick homes and pharaohs' tombs alike.

In this chapter, we're turning our attention to the heartbeats beneath linen tunics and golden ankhs to uncover how these ancient tales of amour weren't all moonlit walks along the banks of the Nile but often complex dramas involving loyalty, betrayal, and sometimes, divine interventions. Dust off your chariot because we're going to explore not just the juicy stories passed down through generations but also how they reflect on the roles and powers of women in Egyptian society. Whether it's the epic ballads sung by lovers or the political machinations behind arranged marriages, you'll find that these stories offer more twists than Cleopatra's eyeliner. Grab your favorite scroll and prepare for a journey where romance and power collide in ways that are surprisingly relevant yet altogether timeless.

Cultural Beliefs About Love Stories and Romance

Love in ancient Egyptian culture was not just a fleeting feeling; it was woven into the very fabric of society, myths, and daily life. Ancient Egyptians viewed it as a multifaceted concept that manifested in varied forms, from romantic relationships to loyalty among friends and family. This section investigates how love was represented in ancient Egyptian mythology and stories, highlighting its complexity and influence.

The Tale of Two Brothers

Found in various papyrus texts, the "Tale of Two Brothers" is a narrative that reflects the values and moral teachings of ancient Egyptian society. Revolving around two brothers named Anubis and Bata, it explores themes of loyalty, betrayal, and the consequences of jealousy.

In the story, Anubis, the elder brother, is a farmer who is married. Bata, the younger of the two, helps him in his work. One day, Anubis's wife attempts to seduce Bata, but he rejects her advances. In retaliation, she falsely accuses him of trying to assault her. Angered and feeling betrayed, Anubis chases his brother away, vowing to kill him.

Bata flees and embarks on a series of adventures, during which he gains the favor of the god Horus. Eventually, after facing various trials and proving his loyalty, Bata returns to confront Anubis. He reveals the truth about the false accusation, leading to a reconciliation between the brothers.

The tale not only illustrates the bond between siblings but also highlights the importance of truth and integrity while addressing the darker aspects of human emotions such as jealousy and revenge.

Love Brings Balance

Beyond mythology, love was seen as a creative force, as Egyptians believed that love played an essential role in creation and harmony and that it was central to the balance of the cosmos. For example, the depiction of the union of goddesses and gods symbolized cosmic order and fertility, suggesting that love was integral to maintaining balance in the heavens as well as on Earth. This perspective indicates the profound respect and reverence ancient Egyptians had for love and how it extended beyond personal relationships to influence their understanding of the universe itself.

Symbols of Love

The Significance of Symbols in Ancient Egypt

Symbols played a crucial role in ancient Egyptian culture, serving as important tools for communication and expression. Aside from being decorative, they also conveyed complex ideas and emotions that were essential to everyday life. The lotus flower, which held deep meanings and was often used in various forms of art, literature, and religious practices, is one of the most powerful examples.

The Lotus Flower: A Symbol of Rebirth and Purity

The lotus flower is unique in its daily cycle. It opens up at dawn and closes as the sun sets. This natural behavior makes it a fitting symbol of rebirth and purity. It was also often depicted in art alongside gods and pharaohs, representing their divine nature and connection to eternity. In particular, the lotus was tied to the sun god Ra, who was believed to be reborn each day. This connection to the sun and its cycle emphasized concepts like regeneration and new beginnings.

For people in ancient Egypt, the lotus also represented another deep idea that went far beyond its attractive appearance. When they viewed the bloom emerging from muddy waters, they saw a reflection of life's challenges. The flower's ability to rise above dirt and flourish reminded them that they could overcome struggles and achieve greatness. This idea resonated with many, making the lotus a beloved symbol across different aspects of their culture.

The Connection to Love

In addition to rebirth, the lotus flower was also a symbol of love, and it was associated with the emotions of affection and admiration. In artworks, it frequently served as an emblem of romantic feelings. Small representations of the flower often adorned tombs and temples, indicating the importance of love in life and the afterlife. By integrating the lotus into their rituals and art, ancient Egyptians embraced love as a vital part of their existence.

The Universality of Symbols

The prominence of the lotus flower has not only persisted through time but has also crossed geographical boundaries, showcasing how symbols can transcend their original cultures. It also indicates how humans have a tendency to recognize beauty and significance in nature. In many Asian cultures, the lotus flower holds special meanings. In Buddhism, for instance, it represents enlightenment and spiritual awakening. This suggests a global understanding of the importance of growth and transformation.

Today, the lotus continues to resonate with people around the globe as a sign of serenity, beauty, and love. Whether in literature, art, or personal reflections, the flower remains a connection point that bridges different cultures and eras. It also shows how universal feelings like love and admiration manifest in similar forms, regardless of time and place.

The symbol is also prevalent in modern wellness practices. In yoga and meditation, it is a symbol of spiritual awakening. Those who practice mindfulness may visualize the lotus flower opening up to signify inner growth and enlightened states of being. This presents a continuity in how we express love and the journey toward inner peace, demonstrating that the themes of purity and rebirth are as relevant today as they were in ancient times.

Practical Implications

Understanding the significance of symbols can have practical implications in modern life. If you're interested in art, literature, or cultural studies, recognizing how symbols evolve can enhance your comprehension and appreciation of different works. For instance, if you're an artist, you may draw inspiration from the lotus when creating pieces that explore themes of love or rebirth. As a writer, you can incorporate the symbol into your narratives to evoke emotion and depth.

You can use symbols like this one in your daily life to express feelings that may be difficult to articulate. The lotus flower can serve as a reminder of resilience and hope during tough times. You could even choose to keep a representation of the flower close by as a personal token of your ability to rise above challenges and stay connected to your emotions.

In relationships, the lotus can symbolize the need for purity of heart and unconditional love. Couples may choose to give each other lotus-themed gifts as expressions of their commitment. Whether in the form of jewelry, art, or simple flower arrangements, the flower can add a meaningful touch to gestures of affection.

The enduring legacy of the lotus flower, originating with the ancient Egyptians, demonstrates how symbols can continue to resonate across time and cultures. With its deep meanings associated with rebirth and love, this flower reminds us of the connections that bind humanity together. As we engage with such symbols in our modern lives, we can appreciate their histories while also infusing our unique interpretations into them.

Poetry

Ancient Egypt boasts a rich tradition of poetry, a timeless medium for expressing emotion. These verses were powerful articulations of devotion and passion, reflecting the cultural value placed on romantic relationships. The poems found on ostraca—shards of pottery or stone used for writing—are particularly fascinating. Their authors often turned mundane activities, like fishing, into metaphors for love, portraying the beloved's grace and beauty in vivid language.

These creative endeavors underline the enduring role of art in conveying deep feelings. Poems served as a means to both celebrate and immortalize affection, ensuring that the essence of love was captured for eternity. This is similar to how we might use poetry or music to express similar emotions today, indicating a universal human experience that transcends time.

In these narratives and symbols, we see how love was deeply embedded in ancient Egyptian society. It was more than just a personal affair; it influenced social norms, religious beliefs, and artistic expressions. In its many forms, it was celebrated and respected for its ability to unite people, inspire creativity, and maintain cosmic balance.

While exploring these aspects of love in ancient Egypt, it's important to recognize how they resonate with our modern understandings of similar concepts. Despite the passage of millennia, the core values remain strikingly relevant: the joy of connection, the pain of betrayal, the power of reconciliation, and the beauty of expression all continue to shape human experiences today.

Marriage Rites and Social Expectations for Women

Marriage was a complicated dance. Of love, yes, but also of strategy and social alignment. Much like a game of chess, young couples were often paired to forge alliances, bolster family status, or even strengthen societal bonds. But the puzzle didn't end there for ancient Egyptian women. Once they had navigated these expectations, there was another challenge in finding empowerment within them.

Meet Layla, an ancient Egyptian woman whose parents had arranged for her to marry Ramses—not necessarily because he was so swoon-worthy but because his family held considerable influence. This was common, as marriages served strategic purposes and seamlessly blended personal aspirations with familial duty. Layla would have carried the weight of ensuring her family's standing, yet marrying Ramses also provided access to a subtle platform where she could redefine her role.

The Big Day

Ceremonial practices, though seemingly just another part of the social panorama, were deeply invested with cultural meaning. Imagine Layla and Ramses being married in a lively ceremony where gifts were exchanged, stories were retold, and ties were reinforced over laughter and food. Despite the simplicity compared to modern spectacles, these rites served as pivotal societal glue, echoing present-day wedding traditions that still strive for significance beyond the "I dos."

The Dutiful Wife

Women's roles in these marriages presented a different narrative. They were active participants in redefining gender dynamics, not just bystanders. So, like a tightrope walker, Layla would have had to balance domestic responsibilities with a quest for autonomy and recognition. Even though male-dominated hierarchies loomed large, women like her learned to carve out spaces of influence for themselves. They developed skills in managing their households and contributing economically through textile production or similar ventures. These activities weren't just survival tactics but tools of empowerment, mirroring the modern pursuit of gender equality.

Untying the Knot

Perhaps one of the most intriguing aspects of ancient Egyptian marital life was the accessibility of divorce—a revolutionary concept when you consider how rare it was in other societies at the time. If she chose to leave Ramses, Layla had the right to initiate separation, offering her a pathway to autonomy that resonates with today's discussions on marital rights. It wasn't uncommon to hear stories of women who, like Layla, could decide to end unsatisfactory unions without enduring the stigma seen elsewhere. This ability to "untie the knot" provided them with choices, which was a luxury not often afforded in historical narratives.

These elements of marital customs highlight the complexity of love and power in ancient Egypt. Marriages stood as representations of larger societal structures, depicting a world where personal ambitions intertwined with communal needs. The strategic nature of unions and women's nuanced roles draw parallels with modern gender challenges, reinforcing the idea that the struggle for equality and empowerment transcends history.

LGBTQ+ Relationships

The concept of LGBTQ+ expressions of love in ancient Egypt might seem as mysterious as the pyramids themselves. But peel back the layers of time, and you'll find that these relationships played a fascinating role in Egyptian society. For example, two men named Niankhkhnum and Khnumhotep are depicted affectionately sharing an embrace in their shared tomb. Were they siblings, close friends, or lovers? The debate around this question adds color to our perception of same-sex relationships in this bygone society.

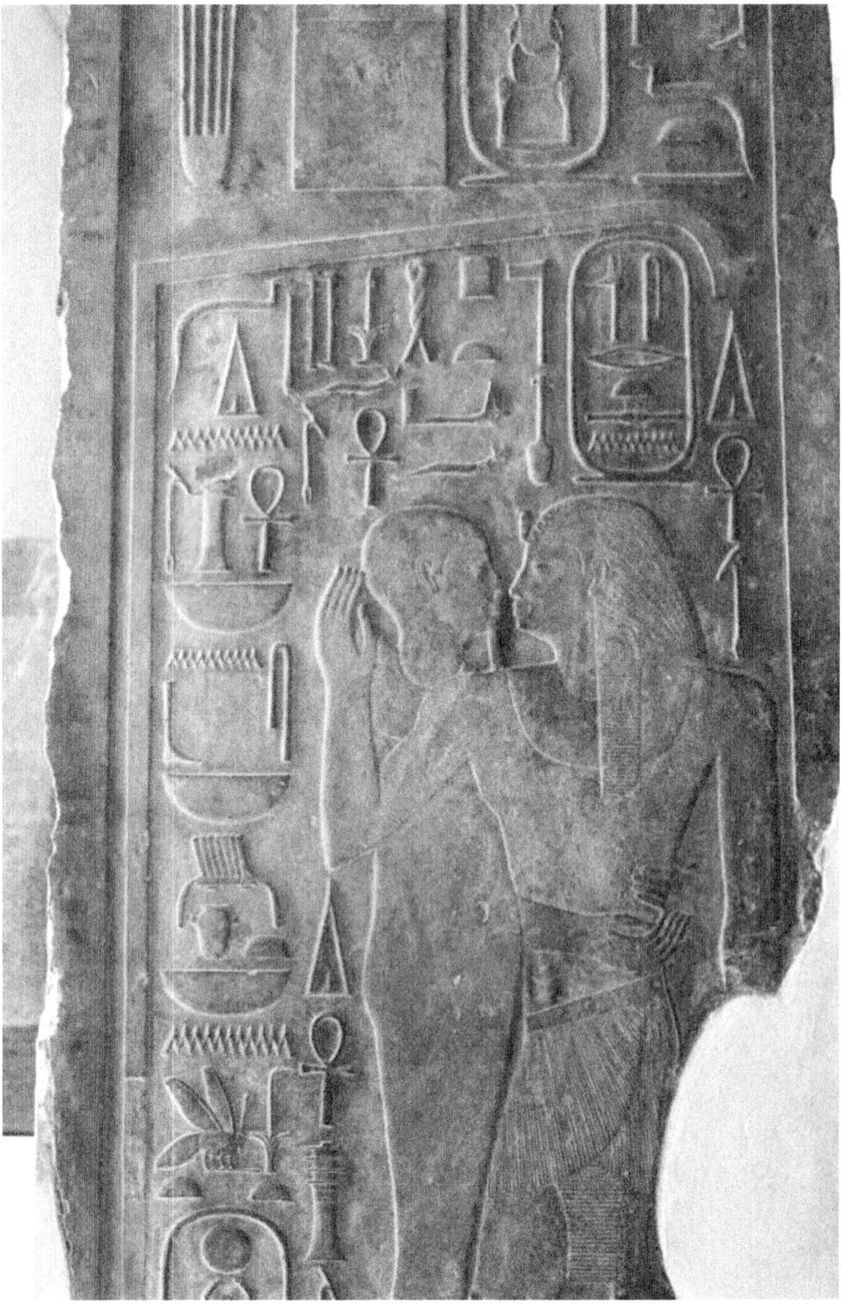

Sexuality Was Fluid

While today we categorize sexualities into well-defined boxes like heterosexual, homosexual, bisexual, and more, ancient Egyptians didn't stress about such labels. They were less concerned with categorizing love and more focused on the background and social standing of who you chose to love. It's possibly this relaxed societal view that allowed for fluid interpretations of sexuality and gender roles. These nuances are echoed in historical texts and artifacts that suggest the existence of same-sex relationships, which broaden our understanding of the past's complexities (Austrian Academy of Sciences, 2023).

Different Standards Based on Status

Public acceptance of same-sex relationships in Egypt varied greatly over time and region. For instance, homosexuality seemed more socially accepted among men who adopted active roles in relationships; meanwhile, passive roles were frowned upon since they were seen as feminine, which was still viewed as subordinate to masculinity. This reflects a complexity not unfamiliar to us today, where social perceptions of gender roles continue to evolve. The class distinction added another layer since acceptance could depend on a person's social status. These aspects provide a historical mirror against which to measure today's ongoing journey toward equality and the understanding of LGBTQ+ rights.

Humanizing the Gods

Divine figures often capture our imagination, and stories of LGBTQ+ relations make these icons far more relatable. In ancient Egyptian myths, deities sometimes displayed behaviors that we might interpret through a queer lens, challenging rigid norms. These examples present opportunities to see history in a new light, one where love transcends traditional boundaries. These stories help humanize an otherwise distant past, showing that the struggles and joys of love were as nuanced then as they are now.

To look back at ancient Egypt is not just to uncover hidden histories but also to reflect on how these stories resonate with modern issues. Nonheterosexual relationships challenged traditional gender norms long before many of the movements of our age gained momentum. By examining them, we invite contemplation on the fluidity between past and present views, encouraging a broader understanding of human connections that surpass time and culture. Although the ancients did not define queerness as we do, their open approach reminds us of the power dynamics subtly embedded within societal structures—a lesson still relevant today (Mark, 2021).

Like a winding river, ancient Egyptian views on gender and sexuality reveal an ebb and flow of attitudes shaped by cultural, religious, and societal factors. Understanding these dynamics can be inspiring when you are exploring your identity and seeking historical role models who embody values of empowerment and equality. What you've learned in this chapter can be a lesson that, despite constantly being challenged, love and identity have always been forces that transcend eras.

Conclusion

As we wrap up another part of our journey through the deserts of ancient Egypt (no camel rides needed today), it's clear that love, romance, and relationships were as tangled and intriguing back then as a spaghetti junction. From the poetic musings etched on pottery shards to the strategic wedding ceremonies that played out like reality TV before it was cool, the Egyptians set the stage for complex societal structures rooted in affection and alliances. Women were not just background characters; they performed a delicate ballet between societal expectations and personal empowerment, much like characters from your favorite Netflix show. And let's not forget those ancient LGBTQ+ icons who swaggered through history, breaking down gender norms like rock stars smashing guitars.

So, what's the takeaway from this riveting chapter? Love, in its many forms, was more than an emotional sprinkle atop life's cupcake. For the Egyptians, it was a mighty force shaping everything from cosmic balance to social harmony. Whether you're seeking inspiration from bold historical heroines or mapping out your career path, the echoes of ancient Egyptian society are a reminder that empowerment, equality, and a healthy dose of romance are timeless quests. So, keep exploring, questioning, and turning the pages of history because, trust me, there's always another fascinating story waiting to be uncovered. And who knows? You might just find the role model you never knew you needed!

Chapter 9:

Stories and Symbols—Women in Art and Literature

Women who produced art and literature wielded astonishing influence in ancient Egypt, creating works much like magical artifacts from an adventure tale. Imagine it: a land where temples hold eternal stories and sphinxes guard mysteries untold. Yet, within this landscape, women's stories and symbols spoke volumes through brushstrokes on the canvas of time. What powerful messages did these artistic expressions convey? The creatives behind these works didn't just sneak around the status quo; they painted and sculpted their way through it with flair and finesse. From the formidable figures carved in stone to vibrant hieroglyphic runes, their work was as colorful and complex as the landscape of Egypt itself.

This chapter invites you to stroll through galleries and libraries filled with stories of ancient female artists and writers who dared to challenge norms through their craft. Prepare yourself for tales of pioneering painters and poets who had no interest in just making pretty pictures or merely penning trivial verses. Oh no! They broadcasted bold narratives that shaped—even reshaped—societal perceptions about gender roles. You'll meet Merit Ptah, whose vivid depictions tell tales still notable today, and explore the enchanting sculptures that showcase queens as much for their beauty as for their invincible strength. These aren't just bedtime stories, girls. They are chronicles of defiance, ingenuity, and empowerment. So, get ready to bury yourself in the rich scrolls of history and uncover how these awe-inspiring women turned artistic expression into timeless legacies that continue to inspire us today. And perhaps they will even spark a bit of creative rebellion in you, too.

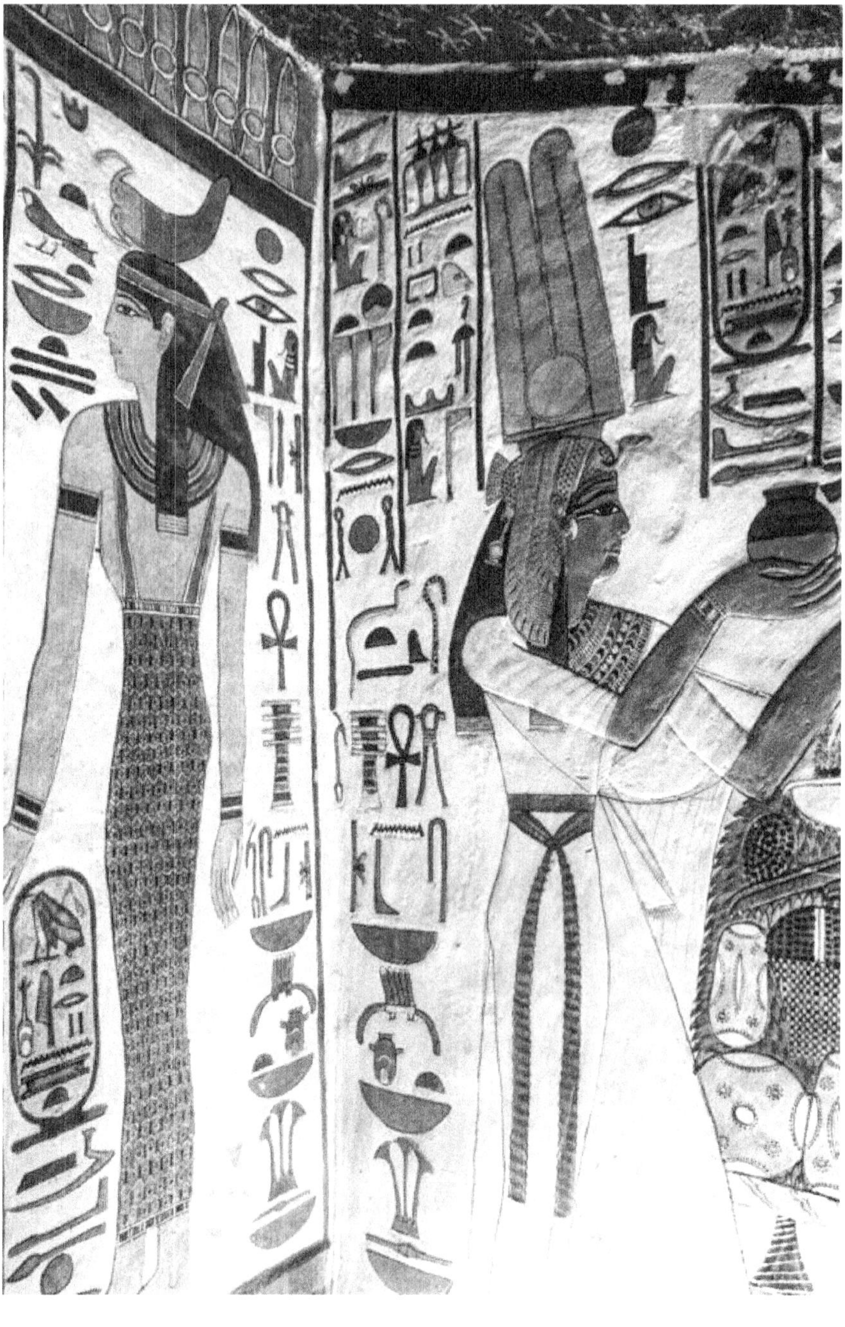

Female Artists and Their Impact

In a world dominated by ever more impressive architectural feats, where men traditionally ruled the art scene, a bold group of women stepped into the arena, wielding their chisels and paintbrushes, ready to leave their mark. These remarkable creatives dared to defy social norms, opening doors in various artistic domains such as painting, sculpting, and weaving.

Merit Ptah: A Pioneer of Female Artistry

Merit Ptah holds a significant place in history as one of the earliest known female artists. She lived in ancient Egypt during a time when women's roles were often limited by societal norms—something you may remember from Chapter 1. However, Merit Ptah defied these expectations through her art. Her vibrant creations depicted daily Egyptian life, showcasing various aspects of culture, family, and work. Each brushstroke of hers has become a vital part of our understanding of that era. By illustrating common scenes, she did double duty by capturing the beauty of her surroundings and conveying deep emotional connections to them.

What makes Merit Ptah's work stand out is the courage she exhibited in her artistic pursuits. At a time when female voices were often silenced, she took the brave step to bring her perspective to life. Presenting scenes of everyday life in art served as a form of resistance against the age-old belief that only male artists could capture greatness. For instance, it's in part thanks to her portrayals that we know women were involved in many activities, such as weaving, cooking, and caring for children. These depictions show that they had significant roles that were worthy of acknowledgment.

Merit Ptah's story is not just hers alone; it echoes the experiences of many female artists of her time. They faced numerous challenges, including limited access to education and the arts. Yet, despite these obstacles, they found ways to express themselves creatively. Women often had to work in the shadows, using art to communicate powerful messages about their lives and aspirations. Some of them also created works that highlighted their relationship with their families, expressing emotions that were often overlooked in a male-dominated world.

These female artists, including Merit Ptah, went further than only challenging the existing norms. They actively reshaped them. They made notable contributions to the arts, proving that women could be influential creators and paving the way for future generations of women artists. Their legacy is evident in the many female artists we celebrate today who continue to push boundaries and redefine what art can represent.

A Legacy of Defiance

The courage these women showed was a quiet yet resolute defiance against a culture that seldom recognized them. In an era when societal expectations restricted women's roles mainly to the domestic sphere, these artists chose to express themselves through public mediums. They crafted pieces that spoke volumes about their strength and intellect, which sent ripples through Egyptian society, impacting gender dynamics for generations to come.

What set female artists apart was their unique perspective. They viewed society through a fresh lens that diverged from the conventional narratives their male counterparts often depicted. Their works offered rare glimpses into the dynamic roles women played within their communities. They captured moments of intimacy, portraying themes like love and motherhood with a profound depth that resonated with all who beheld them. Through their creations, they told their own stories and inspired others, advancing community empowerment and subtly nudging societal norms toward inclusivity.

The legacy of female artistry extends far beyond the sands of ancient Egypt. While modern art continues to evolve, the influence of these pioneering women remains undiminished. Even today, female artists often draw inspiration from these trailblazers, integrating ancient motifs and techniques into their work. This continuity illustrates a powerful lineage that defies time, revealing how past achievements continue to shape current perspectives.

Yet, acknowledging this legacy demands more than simply appreciating the art itself. It requires recognizing the context in which it was created and the significant limitations that were in place: societal biases, lack of access to resources, and general skepticism from male peers. Despite these barriers, women artists made contributions that were crucial to the rich tapestry of ancient Egyptian culture.

Understanding the enduring effects of these early contributions on gender dynamics can provide insights into how women navigate the art world today. By drawing parallels between the struggles and triumphs of ancient and contemporary female artists, we gain a richer understanding of their influence. The presence and recognition of women in art have steadily grown, challenging traditional narratives and encouraging a more inclusive approach to creativity and expression (*Women Artists in Ancient Egypt*, 2024).

The Evolving Portrayal of Women in Artworks

Representations of women in art were more than just brushstrokes on bits of papyrus or chisel marks into stone; they were intricate reflections of societal beliefs and expectations. Similar to a modern gallery, these works were not only visually captivating but also served as social commentaries, evolving with each era's cultural shifts.

One of the most striking aspects of this evolution is the transition between realism and idealism in artistic styles. In earlier periods, Egyptian art leaned toward idealized depictions of women, often portraying them as flawlessly symmetrical figures. Goddesses and elite women appeared serene, ageless, and perfectly proportioned, embodying divine beauty and grace. But as time moved forward, there was a noticeable shift toward realism. Artists began capturing unique features, expressive gestures, and even the imperfections of age in their subjects. They created a more distinct portrayal that resonated with the true essence of femininity. This shift, while still an aesthetic change, had more significant implications. It represented a broader collective trend, acknowledging women's multifaceted roles and experiences beyond being mere vessels of beauty.

Symbolism in Art

Iconography has always played a crucial role in art, acting as a visual shorthand for deeper meanings. In ancient Egyptian art, symbols associated with women frequently conveyed themes of fertility and strength. The iconic image of Isis nurturing her child, Horus, signifies both maternal power and protection. At the same time, a goddess like Sekhmet (who, as you might remember from Chapter 2, was commonly depicted as having the head of a lion) symbolized fierce strength and a warrior spirit. These images communicated powerful messages to both genders, illustrating women's capacities as life-givers and protectors. They emphasized how vital they were to family structures as well as community resilience.

Religious iconography is further intertwined with how women were portrayed, adding layers of complexity to their representation. Goddesses were among the first feminists of history, each embodying different facets of life, from love and beauty to war and wisdom. Hathor, the goddess of love and music, embodied joy and fertility, while Nephthys, known for her role in funeral rites, represented mystery and protection. Through depictions of these deities, art helped shape societal perceptions of women, attributing divine qualities and cosmic significance to them. It was less about worshiping these godly figures and more about understanding the diverse powers women could wield in everyday life.

The Papyrus and the Lotus

The papyrus flower, commonly used by artists and scribes for making scrolls, unites with the lotus to express the duality of Egypt's geographical and cultural identity. The papyrus symbolizes life and abundance due to its use in everyday crafts. Meanwhile, the lotus, as you'll recall from Chapter 8, represents beauty and purity, which are often associated with the divine. Together, these plants form a significant emblem of Upper and Lower Egypt. The papyrus, found in the marshlands of the Nile Delta, signifies Lower Egypt, where the river spreads wide and fertile. The lotus, with its beautiful blooms rising from ponds and marshes, thrives further up, symbolizing Upper Egypt. This connection enriches art by visually merging two distinct regions into a cohesive identity, reflecting the unity of a nation.

The intertwining of these two plants goes beyond mere geography. The symbolism of the papyrus flower and the lotus is profound, as it emphasizes the balance between strength and grace. This is further illustrated in the artwork portraying the crowns the pharaohs wore, which often featured elements from both plants. The double crown, or *pschent*, combines the white crown of Upper Egypt with the red crown of Lower Egypt, harmonizing the strengths of both regions. Artists depicted this imagery to reinforce the idea of a unified kingdom under one ruler, celebrating the diversity and richness of their cultural heritage. In this way, art served as an important form of propaganda, controlling how people understood their leaders and the land.

In tomb paintings and temple reliefs, both symbols appear alongside other motifs that celebrate the life cycle. The papyrus flower often adorns scenes of harvest and abundance, while the lotus features in the contexts of rebirth and the afterlife. This dual representation signifies the belief in life after death. This also relates to women, as the flowers, when used in art, illustrate how women encapsulate both nurturing and resilient qualities. For example, many artworks depict women performing rituals that involve the lotus, showing their role as keepers of tradition and spiritual caretakers. These visual narratives further emphasize that women were central to the understanding of existence, life, and the afterlife in ancient society.

Deciphering Symbols Focused on Women's Roles

Women were often depicted within delicate yet powerful frameworks when it comes to symbols in art. Unraveling them and their meanings opens a window into women's roles in society and highlights their divine status and authority.

The Ankh

The ankh, resembling a cross with a loop at the top, was not just a funky piece of jewelry; it represented life and immortality, not unlike a key to the secrets of the universe dangling from the wearer's neck. Often, it was portrayed as being handed to pharaohs and goddesses, symbolizing eternal life (Mark, 2017). As a symbol, it represented balance and unity, reflecting the union of opposites like male and female or Heaven and Earth. This small but mighty symbol indicated the power and divinity granted to those who bore it, including women, emphasizing their essential role in maintaining cosmic order and life itself.

Women as Visual Symbols

Now, let's explore visual symbolism in art. Women were frequently depicted as goddesses or powerful leaders, affirming their significant roles. Consider the goddess Isis, often shown with a throne headdress, marking her authority and maternal power. Artwork portraying queens and noblewomen emphasized their influence, depicting them as equal to men in both stature and importance. Although these images were decorations, they were also a potent commentary on women's abilities to lead, nurture, and protect. The imagery solidified their positions both in earthly courts and cosmic hierarchies.

Glimpses of actual women in artifacts tell stories of strength and valor. For example, Queen Hatshepsut, one of Egypt's most successful pharaohs, commissioned grand statues portraying her regal splendor. While some depicted her with traditional female features, others adopted masculine traits, asserting her position as a king. These artifacts reflect a refined narrative that celebrates femininity while acknowledging the blurred lines of gender roles and expectations. Another artifact, the bust of Nefertiti, is celebrated for its beauty and elegance, underscoring the aesthetic values and cultural ideals surrounding feminine grace and charm.

Symbols from ancient times still resonate, influencing modern culture and media. Today's art regularly uses imagery like the ankh and lotus to convey themes of empowerment and transformation. These ancient icons continue to remind us of the resilience and multifaceted nature of femininity across time. Engaging with these symbols critically is one way to challenge yourself to consider how they reflect perceptions of women today. It invites introspection about representation and identity. Maybe ask yourself questions like what does the ankh symbolize when it's worn by a contemporary woman, and how does the lotus blossom in today's artistic narratives?

Art continues to be a powerful means of communication, one capable of sparking movements and inspiring change. By examining the richness of symbolism in art, we can uncover the layers of meaning that have persisted and evolved over millennia. The enduring connections between women, symbols, and societal values reinforce the belief that art is not static but a living expression of culture. Each brushstroke or chisel mark carves out a space for dialogue, encouraging us to participate in unfolding a story that began long ago. These symbols remain vital, perpetuating a legacy that acknowledges the intricate relationship between art, identity, and the human experience.

Influence on Modern Art

Fast forward a few thousand years, and you'll see ancient depictions influencing contemporary art and societal norms. Artists often draw inspiration from historical contexts to challenge current gender dynamics and explore identity. For instance, when reinterpreted, the strong yet nurturing imagery of Isis can highlight modern women's struggles with balancing career and motherhood. By juxtaposing ancient symbolism with the issues that we're facing now, artists create a tangible connection between past and present, encouraging viewers to reconsider how far we've come and how much further we can go.

Interestingly, this historical reflection goes beyond conventional visual mediums. It extends to literature, fashion, and media, showcasing how ancient portrayals continue to resonate with modern audiences. In a world where gender roles are constantly evolving, looking at ancient art reminds us of the enduring nature of these themes. This interplay between the ancient and the modern invites you to continue your exploration beyond the pages of this book. As you do, remind yourself that truly appreciating the influence of the past on the present involves acknowledging the importance of viewing art through a lens that recognizes its historical roots and its potential to create current discussions on gender and identity.

Famous Female Poets and Their Legacy

Female poets stand out as unique threads in the history of ancient Egypt, weaving narratives that continue to resonate. These wordsmiths faced a variety of challenges but used their voices to explore and express the spectrum of women's experiences in their society. In an era where social status and then gender dictated an individual's role, women could hold significant influence, yet they still encountered barriers that their male counterparts did not.

Giving Women a Voice

One noteworthy example among these figures was Enheduanna. Though primarily associated with Mesopotamia, her style influenced poets across cultures, including Egypt. Despite often being relegated to domestic roles, some Egyptian women found ways to share their perspectives on life, echoing themes of love, spirituality, and sorrow through verse. Their poetry served not only as a medium for personal reflection but also as cultural commentary, providing a lens into the cultural norms and expectations placed upon them.

Common Themes

Central to their compositions were deeply personal yet universally relatable topics. Love poems from this era, like those attributed to the Greek poet Sappho, celebrated romantic and familial bonds while capturing the pain of unrequited affection and separation. Poetry was a sanctuary for women, offering space to articulate experiences that might otherwise be silenced. In this way, the medium contributed to the broader discussions around what it meant to be a woman.

Spirituality also played a significant role in the themes of ancient Egyptian poetry. With a pantheon of gods and goddesses representing various aspects of life and nature, these works often reflected on divine presence and power. Female poets wrote about goddesses like Isis and Hathor, drawing comparisons between their struggles and triumphs as deities with human experiences. This spiritual dimension not only allowed women to engage with religious practices but also enabled them to assert their voice within these sacred narratives (Mark, 2023).

Influence of Female Poets

The cultural significance of these poetic pieces is worth a mention. Through their work, female poets contributed to shaping societal views on femininity and womanhood. The surviving verses have become valuable artifacts of the past, illustrating the historical importance of women's literary contributions. They offer insights into how women navigated their roles within a patriarchal framework and how they sometimes bent the rules and asserted their presence in subtle yet powerful ways.

Preservation of these works has been an important aspect of understanding their impact on both ancient and modern societies, and you might be wondering how they have survived until now. Ancient Egyptian poetry has lived on through inscriptions on temple walls, papyrus scrolls, and oral traditions, highlighting the desire to preserve female voices. While many works have been lost to time, those that remain continue to inspire scholars and readers alike, serving as a testament to a legacy that demands recognition.

Drawing connections between ancient poets and modern writers reveals a continuous thread of inspiration that transcends time. Historical poets offer a reservoir of inspiration for today's writers, who seek to articulate their own stories. By reflecting on past expressions, contemporary authors can harness the courage and creativity of these pioneers to fuel their own journeys of self-expression and empowerment. You, too, can draw inspiration from such figures and take pride in your contribution to maintaining the richness and diversity of historical narratives.

To truly understand and appreciate the resonance of these ancient poets today, it's important to look at how their themes of love, loss, and spirituality are mirrored in contemporary writing. As we dissect their contribution to literature, we recognize not only their artistic talent but also their determination to have their voices heard against the backdrop of a male-dominated world. It's a reminder that even in historical contexts, where women may have seemed voiceless or marginalized, they actively participated in cultural conversations and left a lasting mark on the fabric of history.

So, when you're contemplating the works of these pioneering female poets, consider the resilience it took for them to create art that has defied the boundaries of time. Their poetry is a bridge connecting the past and present, demonstrating the enduring power of storytelling as a tool for change, dialogue, and introspection. Whether navigating the complexities of love or exploring spiritual philosophies, their words offer solace, insight, and inspiration, and they can illuminate your path as you seek your own place in the world.

Conclusion

As we wrap up this brief tour through the art and literature of ancient Egypt, what's clearer than a bright sunbeam is how these creative expressions were more than just pretty pictures and poetic lines. Our female trailblazers turned chisels and brushes into tools of revolution, challenging societal norms and crafting legacies that refuse to be boxed into history's dusty attic. Imagine a gallery where every painting and sculpture isn't just sitting there looking fabulous but actually whispering tales of rebellion and empowerment into your ear. With a splash of color here and a well-placed metaphor there, these remarkable women showed us how art and poetry can shake up the world, proving that their messages weren't just fleeting whispers but resounding roars echoing through the ages.

So, whether it was the graceful curves of Nefertiti's bust or the fearless depictions of goddesses like Isis, one thing's for sure: The female artists and writers of ancient Egypt were pros at breaking glass ceilings long before it became a hashtag-worthy movement. By weaving their stories into every brushstroke, they gave voice to their passion and intellect, paving paths for modern heroines like you to stride confidently on. As you embark on the mission to tackle your own pyramids of challenges, let these iconic creators remind you that your experiences, too, are worth sharing. So, go ahead, grab your metaphorical carving tools, and be the bold artist of your own story!

Chapter 10:

Standards of Beauty and Fashion

Beauty and fashion standards have never been simple, and in ancient Egypt, they were an especially elaborate affair. Imagine wandering along the bustling streets of Thebes or Alexandria, where women didn't just apply a quick bit of makeup for a night out but put on entire cosmetic productions worthy of an Oscar. It wasn't just about looking like a goddess—though that's always a bonus. Rather, charm-filled eyes and scented oils told everyone who a woman was before she even spoke. With every dab of kohl, Egyptian women were claiming divine protection and social identity like seasoned influencers, all while getting ready to slay their day.

In this chapter, we'll take a good look at the timeless world of Egyptian beauty trends, where makeup pouches doubled as mini museums of cultural significance. As you read on, you'll discover how Egyptians transformed color palettes and wigs into narrative tools, painting vivid pictures of their faith and social position. From describing the heavy aromas of perfumed oils that mingled with the Nile breeze to the kaleidoscopic choices in cosmetics that mirrored inner beliefs, these pages will unveil the layers beneath each extravagant adornment. Get ready to explore how style served as a form of expression and how our ancient sisters wielded mascara wands like scepters, crafting identities and stories that still resonate today.

Cultural Implications of Makeup

In ancient Egypt, cosmetics were used to do more than enhance appearance; they were tools used to reflect identity and societal values.

Kohl

Kohl, a black powder applied around the eyes, served dual purposes. On one hand, it defined those stunning almond-shaped eyes that have captivated people's imaginations for centuries. On the other, it had protective qualities. Egyptians believed that darkening their eyes with it could protect them against the evil eye and give them divine protection, linking the practice to spiritual beliefs surrounding the Eye of Horus, a symbol of health and protection.

Perfumed Oils

Imagine, for a moment, that you've entered an Egyptian court, where the air was rich with heady scents, each narrating a story of its own significance. With this image in mind, it shouldn't be surprising that perfumed oils held an equally significant place in the standard beauty routine. These fragrant concoctions, while keeping women smelling nice, were status symbols and powerful indicators of social standing. The perfumes Egyptian women used often included exotic ingredients not available to everyone. Only the wealthy or those connected to royalty could afford such luxurious products, making them as much a marker of allure and wealth as a token of the divine favor and royal connections they embodied.

Colored Cosmetics

This was another medium for showcasing personal beliefs and links to deities. Ancient Egyptians believed that colors held power. For instance, green was associated with fertility, rebirth, and the god Osiris. Blue symbolized the heavens and water, relating to both the creative and destructive forces of the gods Amun and Hapi. When ancient women chose specific colors for their eyeshadows and body paints, they did so deliberately, making statements about their faith, aspirations, and hopes for divine blessings.

A Shared Language

Additionally, makeup usage was different among the various social classes, shedding light on the societal structures of ancient Egypt. While both the elite and commoners wore makeup, their approaches diverged sharply. Wealthy individuals had access to finer materials and elaborate cosmetic implements, such as eye paint containers made from expensive stones and gold. They turned their makeup rituals into grand displays of opulence and mastery. In contrast, lower-class women relied on simpler, often locally sourced materials. Despite these differences, cosmetics provided a shared cultural language that transcended class. It was a common thread tying all Egyptians together in their quest for beauty and divine favor.

For ordinary women, crafting and applying makeup was a communal activity, making it social in nature. They would gather to grind minerals and mix pigments, creating a sense of community. While aristocrats enjoyed the luxury of having servants prepare and apply their cosmetics, those who belonged to the lower social ranks engaged directly in this artful task, forging connections over the common pursuit of presenting themselves in the best light possible, literally and metaphorically.

Cosmetics even accompanied the deceased into the afterlife, a clear indication of their importance in daily life. Makeup jars found in tombs illustrate how Egyptians viewed beauty and protective cosmetics as essential in facing the trials of the next world. It's fascinating to consider that the same eye palette that was used to frame Cleopatra's enchanting gaze in life might have rested beside her, ready to serve once more in eternity.

Hairstyling and Use of Wigs

Women in ancient Egypt had a knack for turning hairstyles and wigs into a reflection of their social status and cultural norms. In the search for strong historical figures, you will no doubt find the practices of ancient Egyptian women to be both fascinating and empowering.

Wigs

Let's rewind to 3,000 years ago and take a stroll down the bustling streets of Thebes. The Egyptian sun is relentless, but what catches your eye isn't the magnificent temples or vibrant bazaars. It's not even just the people. No, it's the women flaunting exquisite wigs. In Egypt, these accessories were much more than a fashion statement; they were a shimmering display of wealth and style. But it wasn't just about owning a wig. It was how they were styled that truly spoke volumes about who the women who wore them were.

As if cosmetic displays of class weren't enough, hairstyles also varied significantly according to status, acting like a visual indication of a woman's place in the social hierarchy. The more intricate the style, the higher their rank. Crafted meticulously from human hair or plant fibers, wigs and hair extensions were a symbol of affluence. Imagine spending hours in a chair while a stylist expertly braided and crafted complex arrangements atop your head, each plait whispering secrets of privilege. Sporting such a masterpiece meant the wearer belonged among the elite, as specialist wigmakers would weave wigs into elaborate designs using beeswax and animal fat to keep every curl in place (Gattuso, 2022). Meanwhile, those from less affluent backgrounds would stick to simpler styles to convey their humble standing, possibly even keeping their natural hair bare.

Spiritual Significance

Now, let's talk rituals. For many cultures, hair is often laced with spiritual significance. Egyptian hairstyles were rich in ritualistic undertones, with certain styles reserved for ceremonies or religious festivals. While priests kept their heads shaved to maintain ritual purity, ensuring that not even a single strand of hair could interfere with their sacred duties, some evidence suggests that specific cuts and adornments were worn during special rites to honor the gods or seek divine favor (Tassie, 2008).

The practices around hair echo common themes today, an age where self-expression is celebrated. The choice of style often wasn't just a personal decision but was connected to the desire to emulate deities and royalty. Pharaohs and goddesses set trends, and luxurious wigs adorned with gold rings or beads mimicked divine idealism. Back in ancient Egypt, it was as empowering as it was fashionable to wear a hairstyle that was similar to one worn by a revered deity or royal figure, as it infused wearers with a sense of strength and identity. If you're a fan of trendy hairstyles or follow celebrity looks, you might find a connection here.

These powerful displays became a means of self-expression, reinforcing identities and societal roles. Just like today, where you and your friends might experiment with dyed hair or bold cuts, ancient Egyptian women used their hairstyles as a canvas to communicate who they were—or who they aspired to be. Whether through cascading waves of engineered curls or precisely trimmed braids, their choices were deliberate and meaningful.

Clothing Styles

As much as clothing in ancient Egypt was a necessity, it also served as a canvas for class distinction and was a mirror reflecting a person's identity. When walking the streets of cities like Memphis, what you wore told tales about your life, your social standing, and even your beliefs. Among Egyptian women, clothing had a profound significance that went far beyond mere fabric draped on a body.

Fashionable Fabrics

The quality of materials used was a significant indicator of a woman's status. Those from less affluent backgrounds would wear rougher materials, marking their lower economic position. The elite, on the other hand, paraded in garments made from fine linen, pieces woven so delicately they seemed to float on air. This luxurious fabric was not just super expensive but also labor-intensive to produce, a sign that the wearer belonged to the upper class. It was highly sought after, in part because it was breathable and suitable for the hot Egyptian climate and also because it was a symbol of purity, which was often associated with the divine. In other words, wearing high-quality linen was a way to show wealth and, possibly, divine favor.

Designs

Designs themselves became bold statements of status. While the lower classes often opted for simple, functional attire, the affluent donned intricately designed apparel that demanded attention. Dresses for the wealthy were skillfully pleated and adorned with elaborate embroidery or jewelry, creating rich textures that spoke volumes about their owner's social rank. While such intricate designs may have been for aesthetic pleasure, they served double duty by setting apart the elite in gatherings, festivals, and rituals, broadcasting their elevated rank without needing words. The *kalasiris*, a popular dress among upper-class women, featured sleeves and reached down to the ankles, displaying elegance and the luxury of ample fabric.

Wearing a Masterpiece

Functionality versus ornamentation further highlighted societal divisions. For commoners, clothing served practical purposes. It needed to be suitable for work and daily routines. Utility reigned supreme, as garments needed to withstand the rigors of labor under the scorching sun. But cross over into the realm of the wealthy, and you'll find clothing transformed into an art form. Here, dresses weren't just put on—they were worn like prized possessions, flaunted through exaggerated expressions meant to impress onlookers or reinforce the wearer's place within the social hierarchy. A noblewoman might be seen wearing a sheer dress that flowed elegantly to the ground, coupled with a wide collar adorned with precious stones, an outfit entirely impractical for manual tasks but perfect for making a statement at social events.

Beyond aesthetics and function, these garments carried deep cultural meanings. They were imbued with social messages and personal beliefs. Clothing could suggest connections to particular deities, signal a person's life phase, or indicate marital status. For instance, certain colors incorporated into a garment, similar to their use in cosmetics, could reflect religious affiliations or invoke protective symbols believed to ward off evil spirits. In this way, clothes were not only a part of daily life but an intrinsic element of spiritual and cultural expression.

Symbolic Messages Through Fashion

In ancient Egypt, although jewelry was decorative, it was more a statement about who a woman was and what she believed. Think of Cleopatra with her gold bangles and intricate necklaces, each piece whispering tales of achievement or hints of divine connection. Jewelry wasn't just shiny swag; it told the world your status like a flashy Instagram bio in hieroglyphs.

Jewelry and Social Class

When women wore jewelry, it shouted about their accomplishments and social standing. Ancient Egyptians often associated receiving items like necklaces and bangles with important milestones or honors. Today, it would be like getting an award or a merit badge or completing a significant life goal—although their medals were far shinier! These adornments served as identity markers, showcasing the wearer's achievements and societal rank. The bigger the bling, the higher a woman's place on the social ladder. Whether it was chunky collars decked out with precious stones or an elegant pair of earrings, jeweled accessories announced to the community if a woman was part of the elite or a common citizen.

Jewelry and Spirituality

But where there's sparkle, there's spirituality. Adornments carried religious significance, serving as charms for protection or luck. Amulets shaped like scarabs, ankhs, or the iconic Eye of Horus weren't just for show. They were believed to carry magical properties, safeguarding their wearer from evil spirits or bringing them blessings from the gods. It's as if these pieces had a hotline to the heavens, channeling protective energy to keep misfortune at bay. These beliefs showcased how intertwined religion and fashion were, illustrating that faith was quite literally worn on one's sleeve—or neck, as it were.

That's So Last Season

Jewelry's adaptability to seasons and life stages further illustrated its role as a dynamic form of self-expression. Just like swapping sweaters for shorts when the weather changes, Egyptian accessories shifted with the calendar and personal milestones. Pregnant women might have worn specific amulets to protect their unborn children, while others donned pieces according to agricultural cycles or festivals. This adaptability reflected how each person's identity evolved over time, capturing the essence of changes in both nature and personal life.

Artisans Through the Ages

The artistry involved in crafting these accessories highlighted the cultural value placed on beauty and skill. Imagine the effort of threading thousands of tiny beads into a single necklace or mastering techniques to set stones that sparkled more brightly than a desert sunrise. Every bead, every twist of metal, was a testament to the craftsperson's expertise. Artisans showcased incredible talent, turning raw materials into stunning works of art using methods passed down through generations. Their craftsmanship didn't just reflect technical prowess but also celebrated beauty itself—a core value within Egyptian culture.

Moreover, this artistry underscored the societal appreciation for creativity. Accessorizing with beautifully crafted jewelry symbolized the wearer's alignment with these values. In many ways, it was a silent nod between the artist and the audience, acknowledging the mutual appreciation for fine workmanship and the celebration of aesthetic elegance.

Cultural Exchange

Interestingly, the interplay between tradition and innovation in jewelry mirrored broader cultural exchanges. Influences from neighboring regions found their way into designs, much like in today's global fashion movements. Egyptian artisans incorporated styles and techniques from trade partners, resulting in a rich playground of cross-cultural creativity. This blend of traditional motifs with foreign influence revealed a society open to new ideas and one eager to enrich its artistic heritage.

This cultural exchange through jewelry was basically a form of ancient networking in which different styles mingled like a bustling bazaar of ideas, stories, and artistry. As traders journeyed across lands, exchanging goods and wisdom, the fusion of techniques and designs testified to an interconnected world well before globalization became a buzzword.

Through all these different facets, Egyptian accessories served as powerful symbols of individual and collective identities. They were records of personal journeys and reflections of shared cultural values, bridging gaps between past and present, divine and terrestrial, practical and ornamental. When adorning themselves, ancient Egyptian women engaged in a practice that transcended mere fashion, transforming it into a story of beliefs, aspirations, and communal ties.

Conclusion

As we conclude our colorful journey through the beauty regimens of ancient Egyptian women, it's clear that their lives were as vibrant and multifaceted as the make-up palettes they crafted. Whether it was the shimmer of a carefully styled wig or the precise lines of kohl accentuating their eyes, these women knew how to express themselves. They turned cosmetics into symbols of identity, spiritual protection, and social standing. Imagine them gathering in bustling markets or serene temples, chatting away while grinding minerals, mixing fragrant oils, and choosing colors. It's kind of fascinating, isn't it? Their daily routines would fit right into any modern-day salon, where chatty ladies share stories just as colorful as their chosen shades of lipstick.

So, what can we take home from all this glamorous history? In essence, these ancient trends speak directly to our own hearts. Long before today's influencers who change hair colors like the weather or rock rainbow eyeshadow, Egyptian women were the original trendsetters and role models. They navigated intricate rules of fashion and beauty, using them as tools to forge their paths and identities in society. Learning about all of this has reminded us that beyond fashion's fleeting trends lies a powerful statement—an everlasting connection between past and present. It turns out that no matter the era, the quest to define oneself through style is practically timeless. So, next time you're torn between outfit choices or debating another bold hair decision, channel your inner Cleopatra and go for it!

Conclusion

As we conclude our exploration of the vibrant world of ancient Egypt, it's clear that women were anything but passive footnotes in history. We ventured through dusty pyramids and ancient scrolls only to find that the women of ancient Egypt were architects of their own destinies, trailblazers who left their mark on everything from politics to poetry. These remarkable ladies weren't just hanging around and waiting for their chance to fan a pharaoh or two. They were busy actively shaping their civilization in extraordinary ways.

You might recall the tales of Hatshepsut, a female pharaoh who rocked her throne like it was nobody's business, defying norms with such flair that even the Sphinx took notice. Or Cleopatra, whose brilliance and charisma were enough to make Rome itself pause in awe. These women, no mere survivors in a man's world, were leaders, thinkers, and warriors who brought about change with an amazing mix of grace and guts. Their stories resonate with us today, echoing the relentless strength and ingenuity that femininity can embody.

So, what does this mean for you? Well, here's a thought: Why not channel a bit of that ancient formidable female fierceness into your own life? Imagine striding into school with the confidence of Sobekneferu, ruling over your tasks and challenges like the boss you are. Draw inspiration from Cleopatra's tenacity when dealing with life's little hiccups, whether they're as big as invading Roman armies or as small as algebra homework. The essence of these formidable women is their resilience and creativity, traits that transcend time and place. You're more connected to them than you might've thought!

Now, let's bring those lessons back to our modern-day dilemmas. We're living in a world still wrestling with gender equality, riddled with stereotypes and barriers that seem taller than the Great Pyramid itself. But hold on. Our ancient sisters were pushing boundaries long before hashtags and protest rallies. Their stories urge us to recognize our power and continue the fight for equality. They whisper to us, challenging us to advocate for change and to transform society so that gender no longer decides our destiny. Much like these fierce figures of old, we're responsible for planting seeds of progress and nurturing them until they grow into something magnificent.

Your journey doesn't have to end here, though. Think of *Egyptians in Skirts* as the opening act in a much larger performance. Dive into books, documentaries, and museums dedicated to unraveling the mysteries of ancient Egyptian women's lives. Consider it an adventure as thrilling as any treasure hunt. Each discovery offers new insights, about the past, yes, but also about how those ancient lessons can help shape today's pursuit of rights and recognition. And as you explore further, think about this: How can these stories inspire action in the face of today's challenges?

Go ahead and write your own history. Engage in activities that challenge you to reflect on these lessons, perhaps by starting conversations about gender roles and empowerment with your friends and family. Explore the broader implications of what you've learned. What parallels exist between then and now? How can understanding the past move us toward a future where everyone, regardless of gender, has the chance to shine?

Pick up a pen or a microphone, attend meetings, or join groups advocating for change. Whether you're in high school or starting your professional journey, the call for leadership echoes throughout time. It's one that each generation must answer in its own unique way. Channel the wisdom and courage of ancient Egypt's heroines into actions that will shape your world and, in turn, inspire others.

And remember, the sands of time may shift, but the legacy of these incredible women remains fixed in history, waiting for dreamers like you to carry it forward. With each stride you take, whether at a protest, a podium, or simply living out your truth day by day, you add another layer to their enduring legacy. It's time to harness your inner strength, embrace every opportunity to lead, and let your story shimmer with the same timeless brilliance that once illuminated the Nile under the golden Egyptian sun.

Glossary

Ahhotep I: An influential queen of ancient Egypt known for her role in expelling the Hyksos and supporting her son's rise to power.

Affluence: The state of having a great deal of wealth or abundance, often leading to a higher standard of living.

Amun: An ancient Egyptian deity often associated with the sun and air and considered one of the most important gods.

Alliances: Agreements between parties, often states or leaders, to work together for mutual benefit, especially in military or political contexts.

Amulets: Objects or charms believed to possess protective or healing properties, often worn or carried to ward off evil or misfortune.

Ankh: An ancient Egyptian symbol representing life and immortality that resembled a cross with a loop at the top.

Archaeology: The study of human history and prehistory through excavating and analyzing artifacts, structures, and other physical remains.

Artisans: Skilled crafters who create handmade goods, such as pottery, jewelry, and textiles.

Asp: A venomous snake associated with royalty and often depicted in ancient Egyptian art and mythology.

Bazaar: A marketplace or public market, often found in Middle Eastern and South Asian cultures, where goods are exchanged.

Battle of Actium: A naval confrontation in 31 B.C.E. that took place off the coast of Greece between the forces of Octavian and the combined forces of Mark Antony and Cleopatra.

Bastet: An ancient Egyptian goddess depicted as a lioness or a domestic cat, symbolizing home, fertility, and childbirth.

Beauty regimen: A routine or set of practices focused on enhancing and maintaining physical appearance, often involving skincare and cosmetic application.

Beauty standards: Societal norms and expectations regarding physical appearance and attractiveness.

Ceremonial rituals: Formalized actions or procedures performed for religious or cultural significance.

Change advocacy: The practice of promoting and supporting significant transformations in policies, practices, or societal norms to create positive outcomes.

Chisels: Tools with a cutting edge used for carving or shaping hard materials such as wood, stone, or metal.

Cleopatra VII: The last active ruler of the Ptolemaic Kingdom of Egypt. She was known for her intelligence, political acumen, and relationships with Roman leaders.

Commander-in-chief: The highest-ranking officer in the armed forces and the person responsible for the overall strategic command.

Coregency: A political arrangement in which two or more individuals share the power of ruling, often seen in ancient Egyptian dynasties.

Cosmic intrigue: The interplay of mysterious and complex forces in the universe that influences events and relationships.

Cosmic order: The belief in a structured and harmonious arrangement of the universe and existence.

Cosmic principles: Fundamental truths or rules that govern the behavior and interactions within the cosmos.

Diplomacy: The practice of conducting negotiations and maintaining relations between countries.

Divine: Relating to a god or deity who is characterized by supreme goodness or authority.

Divine birth stories: Narratives that depict the miraculous or supernatural birth of kings or gods, often emphasizing their right to rule.

Divine interventions: Instances where a deity acts to alter the natural course of events.

Dowries: Property or money that a bride brings into her marriage, often used to strengthen alliances.

Embalming: The process of preserving a deceased body to delay decomposition.

Echelons: Levels or ranks in an organization, society, or system, often related to hierarchical structure.

Expulsion of the Hyksos: The historical event during which native Egyptian rulers regained control from foreign Hyksos invaders.

Gender dynamics: The social and cultural influences that shape the relationships between different genders.

Gender equality: The state in which access to rights or opportunities is unaffected by gender, promoting equal treatment for all genders.

Gender roles: Societal norms that dictate the behaviors and expectations of individuals based on their gender.

Globalization: The interaction and integration among people, companies, and governments worldwide, driven by trade, technology, and cultural exchange.

Governance strategies: Methods and plans employed by leaders to manage and administer a state or organization effectively.

Hathor: An ancient Egyptian goddess associated with love, beauty, music, and motherhood, often depicted as a cow.

Hatshepsut: One of the few female pharaohs of ancient Egypt. She is known for her prosperous reign and extensive building projects.

Hieroglyphics: A formal writing system used in ancient Egypt that is composed of symbols representing sounds and concepts.

Historical legacy: The lasting impact or influence of an individual, group, or event from the past on present-day society and future generations.

Horus: A sky deity in ancient Egyptian mythology, often represented as a falcon and associated with kingship and the protection of the pharaoh.

Isis: A major goddess in ancient Egyptian mythology. She represents motherhood, magic, and fertility and is often depicted with a throne-shaped crown.

Julius Caesar: A Roman general and statesman who played a critical role in the rise of the Roman Empire and had a political alliance with Cleopatra VII.

Kalasiris: An ancient Egyptian garment, typically a fitted dress that was worn by women.

Kohl: A traditional eye makeup made from a mixture of materials that was used in ancient Egypt to darken the eyelids.

Legacy: Something handed down from the past, particularly achievements or customs that influence future generations.

LGBTQ+ relationships: Romantic or intimate connections between individuals of diverse sexual orientations and gender identities, including lesbian, gay, bisexual, transgender, and queer individuals.

Mark Antony: A Roman politician and general who was known for his role in the transformation of the Roman Republic into the Roman Empire and his partnership with Cleopatra.

Ma'at: The ancient Egyptian concept of truth, balance, order, harmony, law, morality, and justice.

Memphis: An ancient city in Egypt known for its rich cultural and historical significance. It served as the capital of the Old Kingdom.

Merchants: Individuals or businesses engaged in the buying and selling of goods and services and facilitating trade between regions.

Mistress of Upper and Lower Egypt: A title used to designate the queen's authority over all of Egypt, symbolizing unity between the two regions.

Mudbrick: Bricks made from a mixture of clay, mud, and straw, commonly used in ancient Egyptian construction.

Mortuary temple: A temple built for worshiping a deceased pharaoh, performing rituals, and making offerings.

Myth: Traditional stories that explain natural phenomena or cultural beliefs, often involving deities or supernatural events.

Neithhotep: An early queen of ancient Egypt, often recognized as one of the first of its female rulers.

Nefertiti: An ancient Egyptian queen known for her beauty and her marriage to Pharaoh Akhenaten; she is often featured in art and sculpture.

Nile River: The longest river in the world, flowing through northeastern Africa. It is historically significant for its role in the development of ancient Egyptian civilization.

Ostraca: Potsherds or fragments of pottery used in ancient times as a writing surface for notes, lists, and other documents.

Osiris: A major god in ancient Egyptian mythology, known as the god of the afterlife and resurrection.

Pharaohs: The ancient Egyptian rulers. They were considered divine figures who held absolute power over the land.

Peseshet: An ancient Egyptian physician who was recognized as a female doctor and significantly contributed to medicine.

Political machinations: Schemes or plots carried out to manipulate or control political situations or outcomes.

Pschent: The double crown of ancient Egypt, symbolizing the unification of Upper and Lower Egypt.

Pyramid: A monumental structure built as a tomb for pharaohs, characterized by its triangular shape and immense size.

Queerness: A broad term that encompasses diverse sexual orientations and gender identities, often challenging conventional norms.

Ritual purity: The state of being free from impurities or contamination, often required for participation in religious ceremonies or practices.

Sacred duties: Obligations or responsibilities regarded as holy or deeply significant, related to religious or spiritual practices.

Scarabs: Beetle-shaped symbols in ancient Egypt that were associated with regeneration and used in jewelry or as amulets.

Scribes: Educated individuals in ancient Egypt who were responsible for writing and documenting information using hieroglyphics.

Sekhmet: A warrior goddess commonly depicted as a lioness. She was associated with healing and protection.

Set: A god in ancient Egyptian mythology associated with chaos, storms, and disorder.

Sphinx: A mythical creature with the body of a lion and the head of a human, and a symbol of strength and wisdom in ancient Egyptian culture.

Soft diplomacy: A noncoercive approach to international relations that tends to involve cultural exchanges and collaboration to enhance mutual respect and understanding.

Spiritual senate: A governing body in ancient Egypt that comprised priests and advisors, often involved in making decisions related to spiritual and state matters.

Spiritual leadership: Guidance provided by individuals regarded as spiritually enlightened or authoritative.

Strategic marriages: Marriages arranged for political, social, or economic advantages rather than for love.

Stela: A stone or wooden slab inscribed or carved with text and images and used as a monument or marker in ancient cultures, typically to commemorate a person or event or to convey important information.

Temples: Structures or places designated for worship and the veneration of deities.

Thebes: An ancient city in Egypt that served as a prominent religious and political center, notably known for its temples and monuments.

Treaties: Formal agreements between states or leaders that outline mutual obligations, peace terms, or alliances.

Author Bio

Terri Gallagher is a passionate historian and advocate for women's empowerment. She is dedicated to unearthing the stories of strong female figures from diverse cultures and bringing a unique perspective to the historical narrative surrounding their lives.

In *Pharaohs in Skirts*, she blends historical scholarship with engaging storytelling, making ancient narratives accessible and relevant to today's youth. Through this guide, she aims to show that understanding the past is essential for shaping the future, especially for young women aspiring to break barriers in their own lives.

When she's not working or leading seminars for women in leadership roles, Terri loves to travel. While she's on research trips for her books, Egypt being her favorite destination, she can often be found on riverboat cruises to various museums and libraries.

References

Alvar, J. (2020, March 19). *Isis, ancient Egypt's mother goddess, was worshipped throughout the ancient world*. National Geographic. https://www.nationalgeographic.com/history/history-magazine/article/isis-egyptian-goddess-worship-spread-egypt-england

Alvar, J. (2020, October 8). *Worship of this Egyptian goddess spread from Egypt to England*. New Forward Language School. https://vk.com/@new_forwardls_ru-worship-of-this-egyptian-goddess-spread-from-egypt-to-englan

Ancient World Hub. (2024, July 5). *Neithhotep: Egypt's first female pharaoh*. https://ancientworldhub.com/neithhotep-egypts-first-female-pharaoh/

The Archaeologist. (2023, December 24). *New Genetic tool reveals hidden family connections in ancient times*. https://www.thearchaeologist.org/blog/new-genetic-tool-reveals-hidden-family-connections-in-ancient-times

Austrian Academy of Sciences. (2023, July 17). *Queerness in ancient Egypt*. https://www.oeaw.ac.at/en/news/queerness-in-ancient-egypt

Belmonte, J. A. (2022). *Nefertiti strikes back! A comprehensive multidisciplinary approach for the end of the Amarna Period*. Academia. https://www.academia.edu/83716253/Nefertiti_strikes_back_A_comprehensive_multidisciplinary_approach_for_the_end_of_the_Amarna_Period

Chauhan, J., Mishra, G., & Bhakri, S. (2021). Career success of women: Role of family responsibilities, mentoring, and perceived organizational support. *Vision: The Journal of Business Perspective*,

26(1), 097226292110248. https://doi.org/10.1177/09722629211024887

DeLong, W. (2023, April 29). *Inside the tragic life of Ankhesenamun, the wife of King Tut.* AllThat'sInteresting. https://allthatsinteresting.com/ankhesenamun

DeSmith, C. (2023, April 28). *DNA shows poorly understood empire was multiethnic with strong female leadership.* Harvard Gazette. https://news.harvard.edu/gazette/story/2023/04/dna-shows-poorly-understood-empire-was-multiethnic-with-strong-female-leadership/

Diop, C. A. (2023). *Origin of the ancient Egyptians.* Unesco. https://unesdoc.unesco.org/ark:/48223/pf0000156750

Donohue, D. (2024, September 4). *35 facts about Ankhesenamun.* Facts.net. https://facts.net/history/35-facts-about-ankhesenamun/

The Editors of Encyclopedia Britannica. (2017). Abu Simbel. *Encyclopedia Britannica.* https://www.britannica.com/place/Abu-Simbel

The Editors of Encyclopedia Britannica. (2019a). *Ahmose I.* Encyclopedia Britannica. https://www.britannica.com/biography/Ahmose-I

The Editors of Encyclopedia Britannica. (2019b). *Sebeknefru.* Encyclopedia Britannica. https://www.britannica.com/biography/Sebeknefru

El Galant, M. (2024, March 13). *Top 11 famous Egyptian queens: List of names of Egyptian queens.* Jakada Tours Egypt. https://jakadatoursegypt.com/famous-egyptian-queens/

Exploring famous ancient Egyptian symbols and their meanings. (2024, June 12). Sun Pyramids Tours. https://sunpyramidstours.com/blog/ancient-egyptian-symbols

Gattuso, R. (2022, July). *Hair and makeup in ancient Egypt*. Curationist. https://www.curationist.org/editorial-features/article/hair-and-makeup-in-ancient-egypt

GE HealthCare. (2005, April 07). *CT scanning of ancient Egyptian mummies at Bowers Museum uncovers new evidence of early embalming techniques.* https://www.gehealthcare.com/about/newsroom/press-releases/ge-healthcare-ct-scanning-ancient-egyptian-mummies-bowers-museum-uncovers-new?npclid=botnpclid

Gods of Egypt—The complete list. (n.d.). Journey to Egypt. https://www.journeytoegypt.com/en/blog/gods-of-egypt

Hatshepsut. (2024). Fiveable. https://library.fiveable.me/key-terms/history-of-architecture/hatshepsut

History Skills. (n.d.). *Who was Nefertari, the most famous ancient Egyptian queen?* https://www.historyskills.com/classroom/ancient-history/nefertari/

History.com Editors. (2019, June 7). *Nefertiti*. HISTORY. https://www.history.com/topics/ancient-egypt/nefertiti

Holmes, L. (2024, February 16). *The role of jewelry in cultural and ceremonial traditions.* Medium. https://medium.com/@leslie.holmes.writing/the-role-of-jewelry-in-cultural-and-ceremonial-traditions-2208756a8d5f

How the idea of beauty in ancient Greece was reflected through art. (n.d.). Society Reflected in Art. https://societyreflectedinart.wordpress.com/

Hurwitz, A. (2005). *Reproduction concepts and practices in ancient Egypt mirrored by modern medicine.* European Journal of Obstetrics & Gynecology and Reproductive Biology.

https://www.academia.edu/58411774/Reproduction_concepts_and_practices_in_ancient_Egypt_mirrored_by_modern_medicine

Jarus, O. (2023, April 1). *Who ruled ancient Egypt after King Tut died?* LiveScience. https://www.livescience.com/who-ruled-ancient-egypt-after-king-tut-died

Kabir, S. R. (2022, December 14). *Isis: The Egyptian goddess of protection and motherhood.* History Cooperative. https://historycooperative.org/isis/

Khalil, R., Moustafa, A. A., Moftah, M. Z., & Karim, A. A. (2017). How knowledge of ancient Egyptian women can influence today's gender role: Does history matter in gender psychology? *Frontiers in Psychology,* 07. https://doi.org/10.3389/fpsyg.2016.02053

Klimczak, N. (2024, October 12). *4,000 years of sistapower fighting sexism in ancient Egypt: Feminism and the battle for women's rights in ancient Egypt.* Black educator. http://blackeducator.blogspot.com/2016/05/

Kubisch, S. (2023). Oracles as an instrument for political decisions and royal legitimation: A case study of ancient Egypt. *De Gruyter EBooks,* 35–52. https://doi.org/10.1515/9783110676327-003

Lesko, B. S. (2002). *Women and religion in ancient Egypt.* Diotíma. https://diotima-doctafemina.org/essays/women-and-religion-in-ancient-egypt/

Long, A. (2023, August 18). *Bastet: Egyptian goddess, home, fertility, protection.* Legendary Ladies Hub. https://legendaryladieshub.com/bastet-egyptian-goddess-of-home/

Mahmood, P. (2023, March 27). *My husband is dead—Tragedy in the late bronze age.* The Friday Times. https://thefridaytimes.com/27-Mar-2023/my-husband-is-dead-tragedy-in-the-late-bronze-age

Mark, J. J. (2016, April 14). *Egyptian gods—The complete list.* World History Encyclopedia. https://www.worldhistory.org/article/885/egyptian-gods---the-complete-list/

Mark, J. J. (2017a, February 10). *Ancient Egyptian symbols.* World History Encyclopedia. https://www.worldhistory.org/article/1011/ancient-egyptian-symbols/

Mark, J. J. (2017b, March 7). *Clergy, priests & priestesses in ancient Egypt.* World History Encyclopedia. https://www.worldhistory.org/article/1026/clergy-priests--priestesses-in-ancient-egypt/

Mark, J. J. (2017c, March 27). *Fashion & dress in ancient Egypt.* World History Encyclopedia. https://www.worldhistory.org/article/1037/fashion--dress-in-ancient-egypt/

Mark, J. J. (2017d, March 29). *Great female rulers of ancient Egypt.* World History Encyclopedia. https://www.worldhistory.org/article/1040/great-female-rulers-of-ancient-egypt/

Mark, J. J. (2023, March 30). *Women in ancient Egypt.* World History Encyclopedia. https://www.worldhistory.org/article/623/women-in-ancient-egypt/

Matta, N. (2020, August 31). *Sobekneferu.* Ifeminist. http://ifeminist.org/sobekneferu.html

Maydana, S. (2022, March 3). *The war goddess of ancient Egypt: Sekhmet the bloodthirsty (7 facts)*. TheCollector. https://www.thecollector.com/sekhmet-egyptian-goddess/

McGee, S., & Moore, H. (2014, August 11). *Women's rights and their money: A timeline from Cleopatra to Lilly Ledbetter*. The Guardian. https://www.theguardian.com/money/us-money-blog/2014/aug/11/women-rights-money-timeline-history

Murr, I., & Zayas, E. (2022). *Engendering the past: Practices and potentials of an explicitly feminist archaeology*. Barnard. https://barnard.edu/engendering-past-practices-and-potentials-explicitly-feminist-archaeology

Myth Digest. (2021, April 14). *Sekhmet*. Penn State. https://sites.psu.edu/hahh/2021/04/14/sekhmet/

National Geographic. (2019, March 7). *How the rebel queens of Egypt expelled the Hyksos*. https://www.nationalgeographic.com/history/history-magazine/article/rebel-queen-thebes

O'Brien, A. A. (1999, July 15). *Egyptian women in Ptolemaic and Roman Egypt—The economic and legal activities of women in demotic texts*. The University of Chicago. https://isac.uchicago.edu/research/research-archives-library/dissertations/dissertation-proposals/egyptian-women-ptolemaic-a-0

PBS. (2020). *Egypt's golden empire: New kingdom—Hatshepsut*. https://www.pbs.org/empires/egypt/newkingdom/hatshepsut.html

Pearce, M. (2024, April 16). *What you need to know about Egypt's Abu Simbel Temple*. Bunnik Tours. https://www.bunniktours.com.au/blog/what-you-need-to-know-about-egypt-s-abu-simbel-temple

Portrayal of age, gender, and social status in art. (2024). Fiveable. https://library.fiveable.me/art-of-ancient-greece-330-30-bc/unit-5/portrayal-age-gender-social-status-art/study-guide/9CLFe39OyGHRPhXN

SaadEl-Din, D. M. (2023, September 4). *Nutritional health of ancient Egyptians' diet*. Medium. https://medium.com/@dahliasaadedin/nutritional-health-of-ancient-egyptians-diet-837c854db018

Robinson, J.-M. (2020). *"Blood Is Thicker Than Water"—Non-royal consanguineous marriage in ancient Egypt: An exploration of economics and biological outcomes*. Archaeopress. https://doi.org/10.2307/j.ctv15vwjpj

Samir, S. (2024). *CT scans reveal mysteries of ancient Egypt's "Screaming Woman" mummy*. Al-Monitor. https://www.al-monitor.com/originals/2024/08/ct-scans-reveal-mysteries-ancient-egypts-screaming-woman-mummy

Shillcutt, S. (2024, April 5). *Challenging societal expectations: Stories of resilient women*. Brave Enough. https://www.becomebraveenough.com/blog/challenging-societal-expectations-stories-of-resilient-women

Shu, T. (2024). *Cleopatra by Stacy Schiff*. SwiftRead. https://swiftread.com/books/cleopatra

The significance of jewelry in different cultures. (2024). Inspereza. https://www.inspereza.com/blogs/inspiration/the-significance-of-jewelry-in-different-cultures?srsltid=AfmBOoqDc9bSOMnm32mrZaQ9iQ9z1JebD7Qx-E-Ns8_GlYSMn0KX-KOM

Solomon, K. (2024, July 12). *The dual nature of Bastet: Nurturer and protector*. Ars Goetia Demons. https://arsgoetiademons.com/blogs/spirits-deities/the-dual-nature-of-bastet-nurturer-and-protector?srsltid=AfmBOoowM8PC_Fgh22Sdy2opn_cfzeBW9MYAaz8yOFG3QU9qQRI6B_Pd

Talaat, R. M. (2020). Fashion consciousness, materialism and fashion clothing purchase involvement of young fashion consumers in Egypt: The mediation role of materialism. *Journal of Humanities and Applied Social Sciences*. https://doi.org/10.1108/jhass-02-2020-0027

Tallet, G. (2012). Oracles. In C. Riggs (Ed.) *The Oxford Handbook of Roman Egypt*. Oxford University Press. https://doi.org/10.1093/oxfordhb/9780199571451.013.0025

Taronas, L. (2023). *Nefertiti: Egyptian wife, mother, queen and icon*. American Research Center in Egypt. https://arce.org/resource/nefertiti-egyptian-wife-mother-queen-and-icon/

Tassie, G. J. (2008). Hair in Egypt: People and technology used in creating Egyptian hairstyles and wigs. *Encyclopaedia of the History of Science, Technology, and Medicine in Non-Western Cultures*, 1047–1052. https://doi.org/10.1007/978-1-4020-4425-0_9456

Thomas, P. A., Liu, H., & Umberson, D. (2017). Family relationships and well-being. *Innovation in Aging*, *1*(3), 1–11. https://doi.org/10.1093/geroni/igx025

TJ Rumler Consulting. (2024). *5 Inspirational women who overcame trauma to influence the world*. https://tjrumler.com/blog/f/5-inspirational-women-who-overcame-trauma-to-influence-the-world

The Travel Bible. (2024, April). *The art and utility of makeup in ancient Egypt*. Travel Bible. https://thetravelbible.com/the-art-and-utility-of-makeup-in-ancient-egypt/

Tyldesley, J. (2019). *Isis*. Encyclopedia Britannica. https://www.britannica.com/topic/Isis-Egyptian-goddess

Tyldesley, J. (2012). Foremost of women: The female pharaohs of ancient Egypt. In R. H. Wilkinson (Ed.) *Tausret: Forgotten queen and pharaoh of Egypt. Oxford University Press EBooks*, 5–24. https://doi.org/10.1093/acprof:oso/9780199740116.003.0001

Wolkoff, J. (2019, June 3). *Beauty secrets of the ancient Egyptians*. CNN Style. https://www.cnn.com/style/article/ancient-egypt-beauty-ritual-artsy/index.html

Women artists in ancient Egypt. (2024). Fiveable. https://library.fiveable.me/women-in-art-history/unit-1/women-artists-ancient-egypt/study-guide/DnyaMozyQHQdNVBR

Image References

Arralyn. (2019, May 31). *Egyptian sculpture* [Image]. Pexels. https://www.pexels.com/photo/egyptian-scrpture-2402924/

Arellano, N. (2020, September 27). *Brown wooden tribal mask on brown wooden table* [Image]. Unsplash. https://unsplash.com/s/photos/mummy-egypt

ArtsyBee. (2016, November 23). *Egyptian design man* [Image]. Pixabay. https://pixabay.com/illustrations/egyptian-design-man-woman-priest-1822015/

AXP Photography. (2023a). *Carved, ancient wall with hieroglyphs* [Image]. Pexels. https://www.pexels.com/photo/carved-ancient-wall-with-hieroglyphs-16386716/

AXP Photography. (2023b). *Paintings on walls in ancient tomb* [Image]. Pexels. https://www.pexels.com/photo/paintings-on-walls-in-ancient-tomb-18934683/

AXP Photography. (2023c). *Reliefs on ancient building in Egypt* [Image]. Pexels. https://www.pexels.com/photo/reliefs-on-ancient-building-in-egypt-18991526/

AXP Photography. (2023d). *Wall paintings from ancient Egypt* [Image]. Pexels. https://www.pexels.com/photo/wall-paintings-from-ancient-egypt-18934673/

Color Crescent. (2018). *Goddess Isis figurine wallpaper* [Image]. Unsplash. https://unsplash.com/photos/goddess-isis-figurine-wallpaper-RYfZxZwnPas

efuerstenberg. (2020, November 24). *Hieroglyph, light, ancient image* [Image]. Pixabay. https://pixabay.com/photos/hieroglyph-light-ancient-temple-5765796/

kalhh. (2014, March 18). *Papyrus, pharaoh, old image* [Image]. Pixabay. https://pixabay.com/photos/papyrus-pharaoh-old-hieroglyphs-289277/

Lokman Sevim. (2022). *Egyptian mummy and canup exhibited in Museum* [Image]. Pexels. https://www.pexels.com/photo/egyptian-mummy-and-canup-exhibited-in-museum-11156255/

Magdy, R. (2024). *Ancient columns in Luxor in Egypt* [Image]. Pexels. https://www.pexels.com/photo/ancient-columns-in-luxor-in-egypt-21668633/

McDonnell, T. (2018). *Facade of a temple* [Image]. Pexels. https://www.pexels.com/photo/facade-of-a-temple-6322875/

NinasCreativeCorner. (2020, January 14). *Egypt, Dayr al-bahri, Deir el-Bahri* [Image]. Pixabay. https://pixabay.com/photos/egypt-dayr-al-baḥrī-deir-el-bahri-4763312/

19943289. (2021, September 2021). *Nefertiti, Egypt, bust. Royalty-free vector graphic* [Image]. Pixabay.com. https://pixabay.com/vectors/nefertiti-egypt-bust-sculpture-6650993/

spleen. (2018, June 27). *Bastet, statue, cat goddess* [Image] Pixabay. https://pixabay.com/photos/bastet-statue-cat-goddess-3500736/

Varošanec, P. (2024). *Great sphinx and pyramid in Cairo Egypt* [Image]. Pexels. https://www.pexels.com/photo/great-sphinx-and-pyramid-in-cairo-egypt-28682217/

Vika Glitter. (2021). *Close-up of a woman wearing Egyptian accessories* [Image]. Pexels. https://www.pexels.com/photo/close-up-of-a-woman-wearing-egyptian-accessories-10264833/

Printed in Great Britain
by Amazon